lease return or renew this item by the last date shown.
ou may renew items (unless they have been requested
y another customer) by telephoning, writing to or calling
a at any library.   100% recycled paper   *BKS 1 (5/95)*

A MEMBER OF THE HODDER HEADLINE GROUP

sch

Orders: please contact Bookpoint Ltd, 130 Milton Park, Abingdon, Oxon OX14 4SB. Telephone: (44) 01235 827720, Fax: (44) 01235 400554. Lines are open from 9.00–6.00, Monday to Saturday, with a 24-hour message answering service. Email address: orders@bookpoint.co.uk

British Library Cataloguing in Publication Data
A catalogue record for this title is available from The British Library

ISBN 0 340 80472 6

First published 2002
Impression number 10 9 8 7 6 5 4 3 2 1
Year 2007 2006 2005 2004 2003 2002

Cover photo from Hulton-Deutsch Collection/Corbis.
Typeset by Transet Limited, Coventry, England.
Printed in Great Britain for Hodder & Stoughton Educational, a division of Hodder Headline Plc, 338 Euston Road, London NW1 3BH by Cox & Wyman, Reading, Berks.

CONTENTS

HOW TO USE THIS BOOK   vi
Begin reading the author   vi
How to approach unfamiliar or difficult texts   vi
Vocabulary   vii

CHAPTER 1: WHY READ KEATS TODAY?   1
Style   2
Romantic rebellion   2
Life and letters   3
Adolescence and the dream   3
Keats and women   4
The radical upstart   4
Summary   5

CHAPTER 2: HOW TO APPROACH KEATS'S WORK   6
Read and reread   6
Style   7
Ambiguity in art   7
Sensuality   8
Descriptive power and nuance   9
Summary   9

CHAPTER 3: BIOGRAPHY AND INFLUENCES   10
Early tragedy   10
Early development   10
Influences   11
Fanny Brawne   11

An early death   12
Women in the poems   12
The outsider   13
Summary   13

CHAPTER 4: SOCIAL, POLITICAL AND ECONOMIC
BACKGROUND   14
The French Revolution: liberty, equality and fraternity?   14
Victorian values are born   15
The Regency   16
Europe post-1815   16
Oppressive British government   17
Campaigns for reform   17
Religion and moral conformity   18
Keats in context   18
Enlightenment survives   19
Summary   20

CHAPTER 5: MAJOR WORKS   21
Early works   21
Myths and epics   23
Narratives of romance   29
Odes   38
Summary   49

CHAPTER 6: THEMES AND THEORIES   50
Letters   50
Negative capability   50
Empathy and identity   53
Women and love   54
Dreams and the ideal   56

Beauty and intensity   60
Summary   62

CHAPTER 7: CRITICAL APPROACHES: 1817–2001   63
Contemporary criticism: the 'shadow of public thought'   63
Poems (1817)   64
Endymion (1818)   65
Poems (1820)   66
A 'posthumous existence'   67
'Among the English poets': Keats enters the canon   68
Ideas or close reading?   68
Keats's 'anti-romance'   69
Biographical angle: macho man or mummy's boy?   70
Adolescent embarrassment   71
New Historicism   73
Gender studies   74
Summary   76

CHAPTER 8: WHERE TO NEXT?   77
Read the poems ...   77
... and the letters   77
Research the life   77
Read the critics   78
Other media   78
Editions of Keats's poetry   78
The letters   79

CHRONOLOGY OF MAJOR WORKS   80
GLOSSARY   81
FURTHER READING   84
INDEX   86

How to use this book

The *Beginner's Guide* series aims to introduce readers to major writers of the past 500 years. It is assumed that readers will begin with little or no knowledge and will want to go on to explore the subject in other ways.

BEGIN READING THE AUTHOR

This book is a companion guide to Keats's major works; it is not a substitute for reading the books themselves. It would be useful if you read some of the works in parallel, so that you can put theory into practice. This book is divided into sections. After considering how to approach the author's work and a brief biography, David Edwards goes on to explore some of Keats's main writings and themes before examining some critical approaches to the author. The survey finishes with suggestions for further reading and possible areas of further study.

HOW TO APPROACH UNFAMILIAR OR DIFFICULT TEXTS

Coming across a new writer may seem daunting, but do not be put off. The trick is to persevere. Much good writing is multi-layered and complex. It is precisely this diversity and complexity which makes literature rewarding and exhilarating.

Literary work often needs to be read more than once, and in different ways. These ways can include: a leisurely and superficial reading to get the main ideas and narrative; a slower more detailed reading focusing on the nuances of the text, concentrating on what appear to be key passages; and reading in a random way, moving back and forth through the text to examine such things as themes, or narrative or characterization.

In complex texts it may be necessary to read in short chunks. When it comes to tackling difficult words or concepts it is often enough to guess in context on the first reading, making a more detailed study using a dictionary or book of critical concepts on later reading. If you prefer to look up unusual words as you go along, be careful that you do not disrupt the flow of the text and your concentration.

VOCABULARY

You will see that keywords and unfamiliar words are set in **bold** text. These words are defined and explained in the glossary to be found at the back of the book.

The book is a tool to help you appreciate a key figure in literature. We hope you enjoy reading it and find it useful.

Rob Abbott and Charlie Bell

Why read Keats today?

A consistent choice in any poll of the nation's favourite poets, Keats is best known for his sensual poetry, intensely imagined dreamscapes, evocative portrayal of the English countryside and tragic life-story. He remains one of the most accessible of our great literary figures, his poetry melodious and beautiful and full of a warm humanity. And yet, beneath the attractive wordplay, something of the tragedy of his own life situation finds its way into Keats's work – providing a hard edge to what has often been erroneously characterized as escapist, gentle, 'soft-focus' poetry.

Keats's radical stance, recognized in his own day, has often since been ignored; not only did he challenge the accepted norms of his own society but he retains his relevance to today's. Ahead of his time in his exploration of such modern concerns as adolescence and sexual politics, Keats managed to transform his harsh experiences into not merely populist but pertinent poetry: literature which has stood the test of time, beguiled generations of readers and still retained its cutting edge.

Our fascination with this 'boy wonder' of English literature has rarely waned since his untimely death (at the age of 25) in 1821 – and has resulted in a mountain of critical literature. His life has been the subject of two recent full-length biographies, one by Andrew Motion the Poet Laureate, and reference to him remains frequent both in literature (ranging from the drama of Tom Stoppard to the novels of Ian McEwan) and in everyday speech. Lines such as 'Season of mists and mellow fruitfulness' and 'a thing of beauty is a joy forever' are part of our cultural heritage.

STYLE

The beauty of Keats's mellow style is itself a joy forever – its melodious word-magic the fruit of intense craftsmanship and technical sophistication. He took the sonnet form and improved upon it; his narratives and romances combine movement and stasis in a variety of technical forms, from the intense Miltonian **blank verse** of *Hyperion* to the **Spenserian stanzas** of *The Eve of St Agnes* or the **heroic couplets** of *Lamia*. And, most famously, he took the **ode** form to its greatest height in the English language: technically sophisticated, philosophically challenging, but sensually alive – for brevity and intensity his odes are amongst the most remarkable as well as the most rewarding pieces of poetry in the language.

ROMANTIC REBELLION

And yet there is more to Keats than such technical advances. He was part of a great movement in English literature at the time, away from the rational and ordered and towards the instinctive and emotional. With other **Romantic** poets, he takes as his themes ideas on Nature, youth, rebellion, sexuality, the imagination and the self. He brings his own distinctive and youthful perspective to these great themes – often reacting to the work of Byron, Shelley and Wordsworth, and attempting to avoid the excesses of what he termed their 'egotistical sublime'. Perceiving their style as didactic, preaching and strident, Keats wrote poetry which celebrates

KEYWORDS

Blank verse: a style of poetry which has unrhymed lines of ten syllables each and employing the flowing rhythm natural to English. Used often by Shakespeare in his plays and, perhaps in its most sustained grandeur, by John Milton in his biblical epic, *Paradise Lost*.

Spenserian stanzas: poetry consisting of a series of verses (or 'stanzas') of nine lines each with a repeated rhyme-scheme of ababbcbcc.

Heroic couplets: a style of poetry consisting of paired rhyming lines of ten syllables each.

Ode: An elaborately constructed type of poem dating from classical times, where it was traditionally a type of public address (almost like a hymn), which uses an exalted tone.

Romanticism: a movement in literature and the arts which began in the late eighteenth century, championing spontaneous and natural emotions above the rational, the formal, the civilized. British Romanticism is traditionally divided into a first generation of poets ambivalence, resisting any simplistic solutions to complex issues. In this, as in so much else, his role model was Shakespeare whose work (Keats observed) is the richer for being ambiguous on moral issues and dilemmas. Both writers give readers 'space' to work out their own ideas. It is partly because of this (of whom William Blake, William Wordsworth and Samuel Taylor Coleridge are the most studied) and a second generation (Lord Byron, Percy Shelley and John Keats). space that in almost every new reading of Keats's greatest poems, the alert reader can find new interpretations and nuances of meaning. Such richness contributes to the enduring appeal of the poet's finest work.

LIFE AND LETTERS

Keats is generally regarded as the most 'human' and approachable of the great Romantic poets, his letters evincing common anxieties, self-mocking humour and a huge gusto for life, amidst all the 'big ideas'. In recent years, he has been celebrated by literary critics almost as much for these letters as for his poetry. We find in them a fascinating documentation of the development of one of the great minds of his age – and one of the most sophisticated theorists on art and literature.

How was it that Keats could have found such wisdom at such a young age? We must look to the deaths of close members of his family; his poverty and determination and ambition to succeed in literature; the frustrations of his unfulfilled relationship with the beguiling and fashionable Fanny Brawne; and, finally, the harrowing approach of his own death – all factors contributing to his precocious wisdom and the maturity of his greatest poetry.

ADOLESCENCE AND THE DREAM

Unlike the earlier generation of Romantic poets, Keats focuses not on childhood, but instead on the concerns of what today we would term 'adolescence'. This was an area which had hardly merited any literary attention before, but Keats brings to bear a fine intelligence in his depiction of the embarrassments and passions of youth. His own life-situation ensured he was especially alive to the adolescent propensity for escapism – and his best poetry explores the fine lines between dream and reality, the ideal and the actual, tempering an aptly adolescent intensity with a cool distanced self-awareness.

KEATS AND WOMEN

Keats took the view that the fervour of youthful love could not be denied by the increasingly oppressive morality of his time. His legendary sensuality is especially strong in such sexually charged romances as 'La belle dame sans merci', *The Eve of St Agnes* and *Lamia*. In his poetic examination of male–female relationships, Keats often reverses gender stereotypes, depicting strong female protagonists and passive male victims. Such portrayals are rarely simplistic and didactic (it is often difficult to pinpoint any true villains in Keats's mature narratives) but point out possibilities as yet largely frowned upon in his own time: that women might enjoy power. Poems steeped in myth and legend thus provided a framework for Keats's critique of contemporary society – and their very mythic quality gives them a timeless relevance to our own period.

THE RADICAL UPSTART

Many of Keats's contemporaries recognized the political nature of the poet. His work was criticized for its radical liberalism; for its depiction of what were considered risqué situations, unsafe for a general reading public which included women and servants; and, perhaps most damningly of all, Keats himself was pilloried for his vulgar, commonplace background.

It was his own marginalized status as a Cockney interloper in the rarefied Oxbridge-dominated world of literature which gave him his capacity for empathy with the outsider. And in *Hyperion*, the most ambitious project of his career, he portrays the ousted old guard in terms of such sympathy that it seems difficult to remember that, for Keats, such figures of authority had been his sworn enemies all his life. This empathy is typical of his maturity.

Tragically, *Hyperion* remains an unfinished fragment and, like Keats's own too brief career, gives us glimpses of majesty, intelligence and a fine humanity making us all too aware of the huge loss his early death was to English literature. His may have been a quieter, more subtle rebellion than those of his contemporary Romantic poets, but perhaps it is a more telling one.

* * * *SUMMARY* * * *

We should read Keats today because:

- he remains the most 'human' and approachable of the great Romantic poets

- he has his own distinctive stance on the Romantic questions of Nature, youth, rebellion, sexuality, the imagination and the self

- he was ahead of his time in championing a more enlightened, less oppressive view of sexual relationships

- he deals with universal themes of humanity: love and suffering; death and loss; power and powerlessness

- he voices the concerns of marginalized groups

- his style is rich in word-magic, melodious and intense

- he took the ode form to its height in the English language

- he celebrates ambivalence, resisting the simplistic solution to a complex issue.

2 How to approach Keats's work

READ AND REREAD

Having died so young, Keats's poetic output is not as prolific as that of his contemporaries and it is possible to read most of his mature work quite quickly. Much of his greatest work is in the form of brief **lyrics**, **sonnets**, **ballads** or odes. As such, it is eminently accessible: a single short reading of many of his most famous poems takes a couple of minutes. And certainly a huge amount can be gleaned from such a seemingly perfunctory perusal: individual phrases which capture the imagination, thoughts which make us wonder about ourselves and our world, characters who intrigue. But to arrive at some of the deeper connections and resonances of the poems, we need to read and reread.

KEYWORDS

Lyric: a brief poem often on a personal subject or one governed by a particular mood. Traditionally smooth and musical in rhythm like the lyrics to a song.

Sonnet: a poem of 14 ten-syllable lines, traditionally with a regular rhyme-scheme.

Ballad: a poem following the traditional form of a folk song, with regular rhyme-scheme and stanza length, often using repetition and telling a familiar tale.

STYLE

The style, whilst not difficult like that of, say John Donne or T. S. Eliot, can be a little archaic (full of 'Thees' and 'Thous'). A knowledge of contemporary history (or Keats's own biography) gives a fuller context, but it is never essential to an appreciation of the poems. Many of the poems are, however, full of reference to classical mythology or legends, so it is worthwhile investing in an edition with some notes. Such myths, together with references to nature, allow Keats to analyse timeless archetypal human dilemmas. We are also invited to see each work not merely as a discreet self-contained unity, but part of his broader approach to such issues as death and loss, love and deception, stasis and change.

It is perhaps worth reading a poem, a stanza or a passage for the *sounds* of the words alone. Keats was an expert in creating patterns of sound, particularly **assonance** and **alliteration** which he manipulates for certain effects. Map out the **rhyme-scheme** and rhythm, notice the numbers of syllables per line, the number of lines per stanza. Such structural devices are an integral part of any poetry but particularly important for the brief lyric.

> ## KEYWORDS
>
> **Assonance:** the echo of vowel sounds.
>
> **Alliteration:** the repetition of consonants.
>
> **Rhyme-scheme:** a pattern of rhymed words linking the ends of lines together. Typical patterns include alternate rhyme-scheme (abab) where lines rhyme every other, and rhyming couplets (aabb) where pairs of consecutive lines rhyme.

AMBIGUITY IN ART

We are invited to question views on a number of profound philosophical, social and psychological issues. Because Keats deliberately avoids didactic, preaching poetry, he often leaves an issue open-ended and ambiguous. He will frequently include questions in his poems – and unresolved issues, seemingly fundamental to the plot, are open to question. He encourages readers not merely to make up their own minds but to question the whole idea of any simplistic hard-and-fast choice.

When reading Keats, it is unwise to assume that the seductive ladies in such poems as 'La belle dame sans merci' and *Lamia* are automatically evil temptresses; nor that in 'Ode on a Grecian Urn' the poet is straightforwardly celebrating the escapist life of timeless art. Instead he opens up such questions for us to consider – and to ponder whether such a choice is desirable at all; perhaps, he suggests, it is best to remain open-minded. As a reader he loved poetry which was 'Full' of meaning, 'rich' in thought and capable of acting as a 'starting post' for the reader's own musings (*The Letters of John Keats*, ed. Robert Gittings, Oxford University Press, 1970, 1979 [subsequently referred to as *Letters*], 65). Keats rarely signposts his readers as to what to think. The text repays almost endless rereading, always uncovering new levels of meaning.

SENSUALITY

The sensuality of the **images** is often paramount; rarely does Keats appeal, as Shelley does, to mind-created associations alone. There is nearly always a very concrete aspect to Keats's work. Even when he **personifies** an idea, an abstract concept such as Joy, or Love, he tends to give them a very physical presence. Thus in the line from 'To Autumn', 'Thy hair soft-lifted by the winnowing wind', autumn is personified lying in a particular way so that her hair, like the crops associated with her season, may be winnowed or separated. Typically, Keats goes beyond the functional, even as he describes processes of harvesting accurately: he sees the beauty involved in the whole process, the calm pace of it as she lies there accepting the attentions of the autumnal breeze.

KEYWORDS

Image: a 'picture' created in the mind of the reader, often using sensory description. Consistent patterns of images, for instance on the subject of heat and cold, is known as imagery.

Personification: a device by which a quality, or a thing, or a non-human being is described or addressed as if it is a person.

Oxymoron: a type of paradox in which two opposite qualities are juxtaposed in a two-word phrase.

Paradox: a statement which seems illogical, or self-contradictory but which contains an underlying truth.

DESCRIPTIVE POWER AND NUANCE

Hyphenated expressions such as 'soft-lifted' give Keats one of his most characteristic qualities: of being able to modify subtle shades of meaning by conflating two expressions (here an adjective qualifying a verb), thus pooling all the resources available to both. In his best work, Keats often chooses two strong occasionally dissonant ideas, leading to the creation of **oxymoron** and **paradox**. Such devices are necessarily at the heart of poetry which challenges us to see that opposites can coexist – that ambiguity and ambivalence are sources of strength not weakness.

✳ ✳ ✳ *SUMMARY* ✳ ✳ ✳

● Keats's greatest work can be read quickly but to obtain a deeper understanding it requires careful rereading.

● To make connections between the poems we must read as widely as possible.

● Read an edition of the poems which contains such necessary background information as mythical references.

● Despite occasionally old-fashioned diction, the style is accessible.

● Notice the powerful phrases, the hyphenated expressions, the paradoxes, the crafted manipulation of word-sounds.

● Keats challenges us to think for ourselves, leaving many issues unresolved or ambiguous.

● There is generally a very sensuous quality, images being rooted in the concrete and physical.

3 Biography and influences

EARLY TRAGEDY

John Keats was born to a lower middle-class family who had accrued a certain amount of wealth through trade. More specifically, his maternal grandmother was the owner of a large coaching inn in Moorgate, London, and it was into the same business that Keats's parents were beginning to establish themselves when disaster overtook the family. Keats's father, Thomas, died after a riding accident in April 1804, leaving a young wife and four children: John, George, Thomas and Frances.

One of the reasons the family never really recovered from this tragedy was the impetuousness with which Keats's mother behaved over the next few years, remarrying hastily, leaving the children with her own parents and eventually returning alone, only to die of tuberculosis. Another reason was the complicated state of the will of her father who left a considerable inheritance which, if the family had known about it, may have made Keats's writing career a far easier one.

EARLY DEVELOPMENT

After a good education at a progressive school in Enfield, Keats was apprenticed as an apothecary and, after five years including over a year at Guy's Hospital, he qualified sufficiently to practise medicine. However, he chose to follow the path of literature, perhaps encouraged in this by the financial success of such poets as Lord Byron, Robert Southey and Sir Walter Scott. He was also encouraged by friendships: first, with a former teacher, Charles Cowden Clarke, who fostered in the aspiring poet a love of the Elizabethans, especially Spenser and Shakespeare; secondly, with Leigh Hunt, a famous liberal journalist and poet of the day and Keats's hero. Hunt published Keats's early poems in his weekly magazine, the *Examiner*, and can justly claim to have discovered the young poet, recognizing his talent and introducing him to the liberal literati of the age.

INFLUENCES

Not *all* the literati were liberal; neither did the most influential and vociferous amongst them recognize Keats's talents. In fact most reviews of his early work were far from encouraging. (See Chapter 7.) However, despite these setbacks and the increasing concerns over money, Keats continued to write (and read) full-time for the next four years. He was hugely influenced by William Wordsworth, whose philosophical verse together with his Romantic response to nature inspired greater maturity in his young contemporary; by William Hazlitt the critic and essayist, whose lines of thought permeate Keats's approach to literature; by the liberal politics of Hunt who was prepared to go to jail to defend the precarious freedoms of speech in an increasingly reactionary climate; and by the intense verse of the Elizabethans.

FANNY BRAWNE

Keats tended to move around the country looking for inspiration whilst he wrote, from Devon to Scotland, Winchester to the Isle of Man in a series of extended 'holidays'. However, he was mainly based in Hampstead where his house still stands as a museum, dedicated to the poet's life. It was here in late 1818 that he met a young neighbour, Frances (or Fanny) Brawne. His engagement to her followed on quickly after their first meeting, for Keats was infatuated. However, the family finances would not allow for an early wedding and Keats was placed under enormous pressure for his writing to succeed. This led him to attempt poetic drama (a notable failure) and finally to despair. The relationship with Fanny was a cruel one, as he felt continually frustrated physically and emotionally, whilst she must have wondered whether they would ever surmount the obstacles laid in their path. He spent much of that year (1819) trying to stay away from his fiancée in an effort to focus on his writing. His success was spectacular in one sense (he wrote all his great odes, two of his long romances and countless other famous poems), but according to his own terms he had failed: he did not sell any works and he did not complete *Hyperion*, his ambitious epic poem.

AN EARLY DEATH

When he discovered that he had tuberculosis towards the end of 1819, the end of his writing career was nigh. He had already nursed his younger brother Tom to his death from the same disease – which probably led to his own contraction of this common killer. As a trained doctor, he knew that his chances of long-term survival were slim. Keats's friends gathered around and desperately tried to finance a trip to the warmer climate of Italy in an effort to prolong his life. Joseph Severn volunteered to accompany the poet and, after an arduous and often agonizing trip they arrived in Rome early in 1821. Keats died there and was buried in the Protestant cemetery, where his gravestone still bears the despairing words, chosen by the poet: 'Here lies one whose name was writ in water.' In his final despondency, Keats had not thought that his fame would outlast him.

WOMEN IN THE POEMS

Despite the fact that Keats rarely wrote directly about the real world, many elements of his life feed directly into his poetry. His preoccupation with escapism and escapist undying worlds is an obvious response to the themes which crop up in the life and works: death and loss. Keats claimed that he and his brothers could never count on any happiness lasting (*Letters*, 263) – they were continually confronting death in the family. Keats's insecurities regarding women are perhaps in large part due to the erratic behaviour of his mother, whom nevertheless he worshipped protectively. The many goddess figures in his poetry, powerful guides and nourishers, attest to his feelings about women; as do the many unreliable temptresses. Women are nearly always to be feared and rarely to be trusted, the poems seem to imply. Nevertheless he often seems to be deliberately flouting the conservative strictures regarding sex, knowingly crossing the boundaries of what was considered good taste. This was one strand of his liberal sympathies that he shared with his friend and mentor Leigh Hunt.

THE OUTSIDER

Perhaps the factor which gives his poems their greatest strength is that Keats knew what it was to be the outsider. His poetry, whilst it gained a certain amount of literary notoriety in his lifetime, was derided, ignored or patronized by the majority and respected only by a discerning few. To this extent, Keats could empathize with the marginalized and this lends to his poems an extraordinarily warm human quality. Despite his seemingly otherworldly subject matter there is little that is aloof about his work. Empathy and intense involvement are writ large in his poems – and even more apparent in the compassion which pervades his friendships and his letters.

❋ ❋ ❋ *SUMMARY* ❋ ❋ ❋

• Keats had a short and troubled life.

• His relationships with women are coloured by his relationship with his mother.

• He had an unconsummated passion for Fanny Brawne.

• He died aged 25 of tuberculosis, convinced that his work would not outlast him.

4 Social, political and economic background

THE FRENCH REVOLUTION: LIBERTY, EQUALITY AND FRATERNITY?

Socially, politically and economically, Britain was defined during the greater part of Keats's lifetime by events across the English Channel. The French Revolution had at first been greeted with hope by a nation which traditionally valued liberty above all things; but Britain quickly came to distrust the Revolutionaries as the guillotine-fuelled Terror unfolded, as idealistic fervour was replaced by imperialistic expansion – and as France threatened to undermine Britain's commercial superiority by blocking trade routes.

The Revolution of 1789 sprang out of a resentment of the power and wealth of a few, who because of their birth were in positions of control: the aristocracy and royalty, collectively known as the *ancien régime*. The enthusiasm of the early rebels was reinforced by the progressive ideals of thinkers such as Voltaire and Rousseau. Theories quickly became practice as religion was replaced by a form of nature-worship or deism (belief in God without relying on the traditional trappings of the established Christian church), morality – especially sexual morality – became more liberal, and birth was no longer a guarantee of influence. These at least were the ideals promulgated by influential intellectuals for a brief time in the 1790s – and they were often summed up in the famous phrase, 'Liberty, equality and fraternity'.

More zealous and ruthless leaders saw their own opportunities to grab power and quickly France became a bloodbath as first the king in 1793, then members of the aristocracy and any opponents of the cause were sent to the guillotine – in what soon became known as the Terror. Out of this chaos emerged a military leader of great genius who dominated his age. Napoleon Bonaparte conquered most of mainland Europe during a period in which the French, freed of the shackles of traditional privilege, and fired by the zeal of believers in their own republic, established themselves as a power whose only rival was Britain.

VICTORIAN VALUES ARE BORN

British reaction to France's sudden change from idealistic champions of liberty to untrustworthy neighbours attempting to undermine long-established hierarchies throughout Europe was hardly measured. From celebrating a time when it was, as Wordsworth phrased it, 'bliss to be alive', Britain's intelligentsia (including the Prime Minister, William Pitt the Younger) came to reject all that France stood for. If France rejected traditional morality and Christianity, then Britons were obliged to uphold these values the more strongly.

Those who refused to tread this increasingly puritanical and reactionary path were branded as seditious. This changed the whole nature of the tolerant easygoing latitudinarian approach of Britain in the eighteenth century. Victorian values were born out of this desire to control; and this was especially important with the expansion of the reading public. Servants, women and the lower classes were now increasingly literate and, so, what was published had to be carefully monitored.

THE REGENCY

Such a change in morality was of course undermined continually – and not just by revolutionary thinkers such as William Blake and Thomas Paine but by the very bastion of society himself: the Prince Regent. George IV (as he was to become after his father's death in 1820) was notorious for his gambling and wenching, testimony to the hypocrisy which underlay such a seemingly moralistic authority. Liberal journalists such as Keats's mentor Leigh Hunt were not slow to point out this discrepancy; Hunt was jailed in 1816 for what was deemed a seditious article lampooning Britain's corpulent and debauched figurehead. Keats responded by writing fervent poetical tributes to Hunt whom he referred to as Libertas, champion of Liberty.

The Prince of Wales had come to power as Regent in 1810 when his father, the conservative figure George III, was generally acknowledged to be insane. During his Regency, he strongly disappointed those who had regarded him in his youth as a supporter of liberal causes. However, the gap between comfortable middle classes and a working class increasing rapidly in number but not prosperity seemed to be widening more than ever. This was the time of Jane Austen, of middle-class propriety and decorum – even if some of the aristocracy (led by the Regent himself) were guilty of a dissolute and libertine lifestyle. Meanwhile the lower echelons of society, as Keats observed in his walking tour of the north of Britain, were often living in extremely impoverished conditions – exploited or ignored by their so-called superiors.

EUROPE POST-1815

After Napoleon's final defeat at Waterloo the *ancien régime* was restored and royal families the length and breadth of Europe returned to their old privileged rights, if anything more hierarchical and reactionary than before the French Revolution. Keats and Hunt warned of the dangers of these 'sceptred tyrants' who were not placed under the proper rule of law. However, Britain under the conservative Foreign Minister Castlereagh, strongly supported the Holy Alliance of former royal powers – powers who largely swept away the Enlightenment ideals which had been growing in Europe in the eighteenth century.

OPPRESSIVE BRITISH GOVERNMENT

Meanwhile in Britain, the redcoat armies, hardened from battles on the Continent, were, by the close of 1816, being used as a force to suppress the newly rebellious populace. Exhilaration and celebration at Wellington's victory of 1815 had quickly given way to unrest:

* Britain had been crippled financially by over 20 years of war.

* The price of food was excessive.

* Unemployment was high.

* Open revolt was never far from being a possibility for the remainder of Keats's life.

And of course any rebellion, in the eyes of the establishment, meant a full-scale French-type revolution. It was in this atmosphere that spies, agents-provocateurs and troops were employed to try to flush out and extinguish any incipient revolution. In increasing desperation, the government resorted to suspending one of the innate rights of every Briton: habeas corpus – the principle by which one cannot be held indefinitely without being brought to trial. Combined with the right to trial by jury, it is one of the chief restraints upon any establishment becoming a tyranny. Such an outcome was never far from the truth as British rights were eroded over these turbulent years.

CAMPAIGNS FOR REFORM

Events in France hardened the government's attitude to the great thrust of parliamentary reform. Not until 1832 was the vote extended to include the middle classes – whilst working men had to wait until 1867 and women until 1928. Meanwhile campaigners like Hunt were pressurizing the government to include more people in the legislative democratic process. What he and others like him feared was a genuinely violent revolt like the French Revolution and the only way to appease was to follow the great trend of inclusive politics which had been shaping Britain for centuries. Their fears seemed on the verge of realization when Henry Hunt led a mass movement of demonstrations in industrial towns in 1819. These were peaceable but potentially volatile, and the panicked militia at one rally, in St Peter's Field Manchester, mounted a cavalry charge at unarmed men, women and children, killing 17 and wounding several hundred. Instantly, in a mockery of the euphoric victory at Waterloo only four years earlier, this 'victory' for the conservative establishment became known as the Peterloo massacre. It caused outrage in the liberal press and in response Shelley penned 'The Masque of Anarchy', one of the most savage pieces of poetical satire in the English language.

RELIGION AND MORAL CONFORMITY

Similarly in religion, old dogmas and prejudices were strengthened. The old deist ideas which philosophically underpinned the French Revolution were now not only frowned upon but actively prosecuted by such organizations as the Society for the Suppression of Vice. It was perhaps not surprising that classical mythology was so important for the Romantic poets – for here was an area where they could covertly undermine the established official state religion.

There was also a newly heightened emphasis on propriety, precursor to Victorian standards. Thus Shakespeare was expurgated of all unseemly passages in Bowdler's famous and proverbial edition of 1807. Meanwhile, Keats and his contemporaries (most notably Hunt and Shelley but also Lord Byron) were doing their utmost to highlight and make explicit any sexual connotations in their work. They were all roundly denounced for lasciviousness.

KEATS IN CONTEXT

Thus Keats took his place, albeit in a minor way, on what he termed 'the Liberal side of the Question' (*Letters*, 302). He remained passionately interested in the affairs of the country during his adult life, read Hunt's

Examiner avidly and, in his letters explicitly and implicitly in his poetry, weighed in with his belief in liberty – in political terms, in religious and moral. He noted most of the events mentioned above, and observed wryly of the reactionary establishment of his day: 'They have made a handle of this event [the French Revolution] in every way to undermine our freedom. They spread a horrid superstition against all inovation [*sic*] and improvement. The present struggle in England of the people is to destroy this superstition.' (*Letters*, 312). Keats himself suffered under just this 'superstition' as the Tory press denounced his efforts at 'innovation and improvement'.

ENLIGHTENMENT SURVIVES

This is not to say the conservative establishment had it all their own way, of course. Libel laws were continually tested, spies deceived, juries returned verdicts of not guilty, and journals continued to denounce government policies. Open censorship was limited to the most extreme, the most scandalous of cases. More it was an atmosphere of censoriousness which restricted. The Enlightenment of the eighteenth century was not put on complete hold by the aftermath of the French Revolution. Indeed in science and industry, innovation and invention were extremely rapid over Keats's lifetime as the Industrial Revolution changed the face of British society. Manufacturers, such as Josiah Wedgwood, found ever cheaper more efficient ways to turn raw materials (many of them garnered from the colonies) into finished products for British and (increasingly) European markets.

Science also thrived as Keats would have been most aware. He was taught by one of the leading medical minds of the age, Sir Astley Cooper. Other notable scientists, prominent in an age which saw science reach a much wider reading public, included Sir Humphrey Davy (friend of Coleridge) and Joseph Priestley.

Above all, this was one of the great ages of English literature. Whilst Walter Scott and Jane Austen were writing novels still read and studied today, the Romantic poets were composing some of the greatest verse the nation has ever produced. It seems that, despite the atmosphere of fear and uncertainty, conditions were excellent for great writers to flourish.

---

* * *SUMMARY* * *

- Britain became more reactionary in response to the French Revolution.

- Moral certainties and 'Victorian values' were born in this era.

- The establishment opposed any movement for progress.

- Government used laws and troops to suppress its people.

- Any deviant literature – either sexually explicit or condemning the establishment – was condemned or suppressed.

- Nevertheless the fight for liberty continued.

EARLY WORKS

Keats was 18 when he began writing poetry and, like most poets, his first attempts were imitations. His role models included the Elizabethan poet Spenser, Milton, Lord Byron and Leigh Hunt. Promising lines here and there impressed friends and critics enough to encourage his future development. He chose various forms, experimenting with heroic couplets, Spenserian stanzas, the ode and the lyric.

'On First Looking into Chapman's Homer'

Keats's favourite early form was the sonnet, the most successful of which celebrates his reading of other poets. 'On First Looking into Chapman's Homer' pays tribute to the work of two writers: the ancient Greek **epic** poet, Homer, and the Elizabethan poet, George Chapman, who translated Homer into English.

> ## KEYWORD
>
> Epic: A long poem, detailing great heroic deeds. Some of the earliest recorded examples of this form are Homer's *The Iliad* and *The Odyssey*.

One night he was shown a very rare folio edition of Chapman's translation by his friend and mentor, Charles Cowden Clarke. They read with growing excitement until about dawn when Keats departed. By ten o'clock the next morning Keats had sent the completed sonnet to his friend, and it remains, justifiably, one of his most famous poems.

The sonnet is a succinct and very clear statement by Keats of his taste in poetry. The most popular and available translation of Homer at this time was by Alexander Pope, a poet who seemed to stand for everything that was rational, orderly and controlled. Pope favoured and perfected the heroic couplet: he produced witty, epigrammatic and often highly satirical works, consisting almost entirely of balanced, self-contained units of thought – to which the heroic couplet leant itself splendidly. Elsewhere, Keats described the excessive use of this device as resembling a 'rocking horse', in its facile reduction of the natural spontaneity of poetry to a sing-song rhythm which can be taught and copied like the work of 'handicraftsmen' ('Sleep and Poetry', 186, 200).

Thus, when Keats writes about Chapman's translation as 'speak[ing] out loud and bold' he is making a clear distinction between this robust style and what he considered the tamer version available in Pope's work. Keats claims he had never felt able to enter the 'wide expanse' of Homer's world until Chapman gave him the key.

The whole sonnet is an extended **metaphor** based on the discovery of the New World by the early explorers or the detection of new planets by astronomers. The poem builds up from a steady beginning to a breathless climax which perfectly captures the sense of wonder of the pioneer. And despite the fact that Homer's epics had been more discussed, read and pondered over than any other European

> **KEYWORD**
>
> Metaphor: the opposite of the literal. A comparison which instead of stating outright that something is *like* something else (as a simile does), *implies* the comparison by identifying the two things. When Keats says that he has 'travel'd in the realms of gold' he does not mean literal travel but metaphorical; he has read widely in the rich 'realms' of literature.

literature, that is exactly how Keats felt on reading Chapman's translation.

MYTHS AND EPICS

It was no surprise that Keats and his friends turned to Homer for inspiration. The current fashion was to regard the epic as the zenith of the poet's career, the chief test of his invention. Milton was the English role model whom all the Romantic poets regarded with awe. Wordsworth's response was 'The Prelude' whilst Coleridge prepared himself for a work which he would never write.

Keats's attempt at the epic also foundered: his first work, *Endymion*, was not a critical success, but his incomplete poem, *Hyperion* impressed his contemporaries, with even the scathing Byron regarding it with awe. It has a grandeur and a sense of scale which often rivals Milton's *Paradise Lost* in its sense of portentous doom.

Endymion

Endymion was written in 1817 and published the following year. Subtitled 'A Poetic Romance', the poem takes a very slight story, that of the mortal Endymion who is wooed secretly by the moon-goddess Diana, and embellishes furiously for 4000 lines. Many of these lines are excellent; many are at best forgettable. The narrative force is often entirely lacking, although the thought is occasionally interesting and highly political. At the beginning of the third book, Keats makes a savage attack on the Regency establishment and other post-Napoleonic European governments, for their conservative, self-serving and blind approach to power, religion and the 'blown self-applause' of contemporary politics.

Some set-piece lyrics embedded in the poem are justly famous: 'O Sorrow' from the fourth book is a touching piece and the 'Hymn to Pan' is a strong evocation of a pre-Christian natural religion which Keats felt very much at home with. Most of the poem is in very loose heroic couplets, characterized by very strong **enjambment** as Keats continued in his efforts to escape the constraints of tight controlled **end-stopped Augustan** poetry.

The most famous lines are perhaps the opening ones where Keats set out his anti-utilitarian creed of beauty: 'A thing of beauty is a joy for ever'; any experience of the aesthetic creates a mental sanctuary, keeping 'a bower quiet for us' – a haven away from the harsh reality of modern life.

In *Endymion* Keats attempts to create just such a 'bower' – a mysterious netherworld full of gems, flowers, adolescent moodswings and nebulous solutions. The philosophy behind this search for an ideal is a little confused – some commentators finding evidence of neoplatonic rejection of the real world, others focusing on the slightly risqué sexual encounters depicted in the poem, with any number of nymphs, goddesses and dusky maidens meeting our bemused hero on his search for the goddess of his dreams. Adolescent fantasy or adult philosophy? Perhaps it is fair to Keats to say that, as with

KEYWORDS

Enjambment: a French word which describes the running on of one line of poetry into another, providing a sense of continuity, spontaneity and freedom.

End-stopped: the opposite of enjambment; here the sense of the sentence requires a pause at the end of each line or couplet, giving a sense of containment, structure and order.

Augustan: an era of English literature characterized by a reverence for all things classical, particularly the Latin literature of that period in Roman history when Augustus Caesar ruled (27 BC–AD 14). The English Augustans of the early to mid- eighteenth century favoured heroic couplets and well ordered verse.

nearly all his work, the neutral approach is the most successful – that is, there are many strands to the work, which he composed over several months as, like his hero, he embarked on a voyage of discovery.

Hyperion

Keats claimed in the preface to *Endymion* that he hoped he had not 'in too late a day touched the beautiful mythology of Greece, and dulled its brightness: for I wish to try once more, before I bid it farewell'. Already he had in mind the great epic for which this had been merely a preparatory trial. Within a year, in one of the most astonishing maturations of English literature, Keats had begun *Hyperion* – still in the world of Greek myth but so far removed from the callow floweriness of *Endymion* as to seem the work of another poet. Where the first poem had been largely mocked by the critics (Byron described it as 'shabby genteel' poetry) often because of Keats's presumption in invading the territory of the upper classes, *Hyperion* brought almost universal approbation. Even Byron termed it 'sublime as Aeschylus' – a tribute to Keats's empathic reconstruction of an ancient Classical style. (Byron, *Works: Letters and Journals*, ed. R.E. Prothero, 6 vols, 1898–1901, V, 588; cited W. J. Bate, John Keats, Harvard University Press, 1963, 409).

The story is based on Greek myth and is set at the point when Zeus and his fellow Olympian gods take command, at the expense of the older generation who had attempted to withhold power. Zeus's father Saturn is pictured at the opening of Keats's epic in absolute despair, failing to understand why he had to lose his realm. Of the same generation as Saturn, Hyperion has yet to give sway to the new Olympians. But this is less to do with his own heroism than with the gradual preparation of the Olympian who is fated to supplant him as god of the sun. In the fragmentary third book of the poem we finally meet Apollo who is destined for greatness at Hyperion's expense.

That we focus on those who have lost power rather than the all-conquering Zeus, is typical of Keats's tendency to empathize. For his political persuasions might lead us to expect him to have little time for an *ancien régime* whose time has gone – one who clung selfishly and short-sightedly to power. Indeed Keats describes one of their number, Oceanus, taking the side of the new generation claiming that change and improvement is inevitable. But it is with Saturn, the massively despondent tragic figure of the opening of the poem, that our sympathies lie.

Instead of the chirping contrived rhymes of *Endymion*, Hyperion has mature blank verse, often intricately stitched together with patterns of assonance and alliteration which repay the closest scrutiny. The opening lines are a masterstroke in sustained negation as Saturn is depicted as 'Far from the fiery noon', removed from all influence, his 'old right hand … nerveless, listless, dead, / Unsceptered' (III, 18–19). With his 'realmless eyes' Saturn looks up to see the goddess Thea who eventually persuades him to meet the other defeated Titans.

The second book opens with a description of the 'den' where the Titans are hiding

> like a dismal cirque
> Of Druid stones upon a forlorn moor
>
> (II, 34–6)

The images are superbly statuesque and yet suggestive of enormous power if unleashed and channelled properly:

> Creus was one; his ponderous iron mace
> Lay by him, and a shattered rib of rock
> Told of his rage, ere he thus sank and pined.
>
> (II, 41–3)

Hyperion is full of these moments of grandeur and power as the defeated Titans are already 'hurling mountains' in their vengeful imaginations (II, 70). To Saturn's impassioned plea for advice in this dire loss, Oceanus replies that they must accept the new generation: 'For 'tis the eternal law/ That first in beauty shall be first in might.' (II, 228–9). Just as Enceladus is gainsaying such defeatism and rousing the Titans to revenge, Hyperion arrives, the glorious 'King of Day' (II, 380). But instead of instilling hope, Hyperion seems to encapsulate the 'Despondence' of those gathered around him. For it is as if they see in his 'dejected' countenance a foretaste of his own defeat and a reflection of their own.

If the poem is a general disquisition on what Keats termed the 'grand march of intellect' (*Letters*, 96) it is also, to a lesser extent, a personal response to pain and grief. The original version of *Hyperion* was composed in the autumn and winter of 1818 whilst Keats was nursing his brother Tom to his death. Typically, Keats used the poem as both an escape from this excruciating time and a way of expressing some of the pain. He wrote to a friend, saying, '[Tom's] identity presses upon me so ... I am obliged to write and plunge into abstract images' (*Letters*, 153). Abstract or removed the images may have been, but mythical or not, some of the physical and emotional pain he described in the Titans has the ring of truth about it.

A very different mood is created in the fragmentary final book – a mood much closer to *Endymion* than anything so far in the poem. In a world full of bowers and nymphs, of rivulets and flowers, Apollo awakens and meets the goddess Mnemosyne who oversees his apotheosis into the new sun god – at which point the poem abruptly closes. What is interesting about this metamorphosis is that it is through his knowledge of, and insight into, human suffering that Apollo takes up his power.

> Knowledge enormous makes a God of me.
> Names, deeds, gray legends, dire events, rebellions,
> Majesties, sovran voices, agonies,
> Creations and destroyings, all at once
> Pour into the wide hollows of my brain,
> Deify me ...
>
> (III, 113–18)

As well as being sun-god, Apollo was the god of poetry as well: Keats is thus suggesting that for the poet, as for the ruler, empathy is the key. Those who, by imagination, can know what it is to experience the extremes of sorrow and joy are fit to write or to rule. The narrower imaginations of the Titans, most of whom are trapped in their own personal woes, mean that they are less fit for power. Keats, who knew full well how self-serving and small-minded both the politicians and many of the writers of his day were, is thus writing about ideals rather than reality.

Thus Keats's hero, like Endymion in the earlier work, is an adolescent on the verge of power. Though seemingly a weak character, who passively responds to events rather than creating them, his very lack of moral certitude is a challenge to increasingly strict moral principles. Far from forming his downfall, Endymion's love of pleasure, his quest to find the object of his 'improper' dreams form a mode of salvation in the scheme of the poem.

Another form of challenge to the establishment was the use of Greek myth at all. Unlike the heroes of these poems, Keats's claim to a place amongst the elite of society was hardly strong. His education was not as extensive as those of his contemporaries who had attended Oxford or Cambridge, and the critics of the time made a great issue of his presumption in writing about Greek myth at all. The classics were the preserve of the elite and yet Keats, far from pretending to be well educated, had advertised his ignorance of Greek in one of his first published pieces, 'On First Looking into Chapman's Homer'.

He self-confessedly relied on translations. Why then trespass on this preserve of the rich? Several reasons dovetailed into his choice of subject matter. First, the classical myths had been a favoured source for his own favourite poets, the Elizabethans. Secondly, there was a huge upsurge in interest in Greek, as opposed to Roman, culture towards the end of the century. Partly this was aesthetic with the recent work of such scholars as Winckelmann, Herder and Schlegel being enlivened in London by the arrival of Lord Elgin's marbles taken from the Athenian Acropolis in 1812. But the Hellenic revival was also politically inspired as first the American and then the French Revolutions revived ideas of the earliest democratic state in Athens. This Hellenic revival ('We are all Greeks' claimed Shelley in the introduction to his poem *Hellas*) was further fuelled by the supposed relative freedom of ancient Greek civilizations in all matters sexual. The myths often describe a much more liberated society – and referring to nymphs and goddesses was often the only way a young Regency poet could depict any explicit sexual content.

NARRATIVES OF ROMANCE

If *Hyperion* was composed under the stress of Tom's final illness, the narratives to which Keats next turned were a response to happier circumstances. Early in 1819, he began a series of romances which have remained among his most popular poems. It is perhaps a little trite to claim that his relationship with Frances Brawne was directly responsible for these poems, but the whole complex of feelings which their relationship engendered certainly feeds into these multifaceted tales of love and betrayal, beauty and oppression. It was not the first time that Keats had written romances. *Endymion* has been subtitled 'a romance', and Keats's second major attempt at the genre was *Isabella; or the Pot of Basil*, written in the spring of 1818. But Keats came to look back on both as rather callow 'mawkish' poems with 'too much inexperience of life' about them (Preface to *Endymion*; *Letters*, 298).

Isabella: or the Pot of Basil

'Isabella' concerns a young man, Lorenzo, of too lowly a background to become attached to the fair Isabella. He is murdered by her oppressive older brothers but she finds his buried body after a visionary dream and then, in a rather gruesomely described episode, retrieves his dismembered head which she conceals in a pot of basil. She weeps and mourns for him for the rest of her life, her grief causing insanity.

The story is taken from the medieval Italian writer, Boccaccio and embellished by many poetical and rhetorical flourishes. The contrast between the flowery starry-eyed romance of the opening and the grim 'wormy circumstance' (385) of the discovery of the corpse is stark – and not a little sensationalist. Keats had not yet discovered the right balance between delight and melancholy which was to characterize his greatest work.

His choice of tale, however, is revealing. The youth who is denied access to the lover is the very stuff of romance, but it has special resonance for Keats, who keenly felt his lack of social status, wealth and influence, and constantly felt excluded from society's centre. He was acutely aware of his lack of appeal to women – but more especially to their families, because of his lack of prospects. His choice of career as a writer did not bring with it any secure hopes of future wealth or security.

The Eve of St Agnes

The hero of his next romance, *The Eve of St Agnes*, is similarly excluded from the object of his dreams. Porphyro tentatively approaches the castle where the beautiful Madeline lies sleeping, knowing that if he is discovered the brutal baron and his 'hot-blooded lords' (86) will attack him as an enemy of inferior 'lineage' (88): a similarly gruesome fate to that meeting Lorenzo in 'Isabella'. However, by the time Keats began writing *The Eve* in January 1819, 'inexperience of life' had been replaced by the first flushes of real love in his own life. He had met Frances (or Fanny) Brawne in the autumn of 1818 and it seems finally declared his love at Christmas. The knowledge of the vicissitudes of a real romantic relationship feeds into his homage to young love.

The poem is based on a medieval superstition, that if a maiden fasted on the 21 January (St Agnes' Eve), she might dream of her future husband. The superstition's emphasis on 'visions' must have appealed to Keats, and he created a scenario whereby the dream came true in a very immediate sense for Madeline. What he also liked about the legend was the distinction between and yet interdependence of abstinence and sensuality – the 'visions of delight' depend upon the 'supperless' self-denial.

Keats took this paradox and made the framework of the entire poem from it. We are made to wait for the 'honey'd middle' of the poem, the sweet centre, full of warmth and sensual fulfilment. Before this there are not only the delaying 'ceremonies due' performed by Madeline, not only the risks undertaken by Porphyro, but the introductory prologue concerning a beadsman. Keats chose as his setting a suitably medieval, and therefore Roman Catholic, backdrop. A beadsman is a poor retainer, employed by the rich to say prayers on their behalf. The contrast between rich and poor is deliberately heightened by Keats as, whilst this 'patient holy man' is saying his prayers, counting the beads on his rosary with 'numb' fingers, the Baron and his 'thousand guests' are enjoying the revelries of a medieval midwinter banquet. Occasional strains of the revelry ('silver, snarling trumpets' [31]) waft through as a background noise to the quieter ceremonies first of the Beadsman, then the retiring Madeline.

The inclusion of the Beadsman is a framing device – his death ('for aye unsought for ... among his ashes cold' [378]) rounds off the poem completing a cold, self-denying and pious frame to highlight the warm, self-indulgent and yet holy picture which Keats places at the heart of his poem.

As in 'Isabella', we are confronted by a self-serving, bullying elite; but whereas in the earlier poem the brothers are exaggerated, almost pantomime villains, the Baron and his cronies are vaguely sketched and therefore more menacing. Because we never actually see them directly they retain not only the element of rumoured brutality, but, conversely, the possibility of being rounded characters, capable of virtue as well as villainy.

Such is certainly the case with Keats's hero Porphyro. Having braved the cruel elements 'across the moors' and the even crueller revellers within the castle, Porphyro arrives into the poem as the archetypal hero, 'with heart on fire /For Madeline' – already the suggestions in his name (meaning purple) are reinforced by the imagery of warmth which he brings into the cold world of the poem. But this hotheaded impetuousness also introduces a more sinister element to the poem as he suddenly has the idea of sharing in Madeline's magical evening. He meets a 'beldame', an old servant, called Angela. When she tells Porphyro that Madeline is performing the ceremonies of St Agnes' Eve he persuades her to let him into Madeline's bedchamber to witness her 'vision'. Of course, when he sees her retire to bed (and her erotically charged disrobing is memorable for Keats's intense sensuousness), he has other ideas and resolves to become the living incarnation of her dream. Although Madeline is soon persuaded to elope with her ardent lover and they escape into the storm, this 'hoodwinking' of Madeline is an issue which has troubled readers and critics such as Jack Stillinger (see Chapter 7).

Thus summarized the story is slight. The power of the poem lies in the highly charged atmosphere around the bedroom: the stained-glass window which overlooks the scene, 'blush[ing] with blood of queens and kings' (216); the feast which Porphyro makes for himself full of exotic fruits 'From silken Samarcand to cedar'd Lebanon' (270); and above all Porphyro's presence and his reactions which we are constantly reminded of throughout the description as he 'gazed upon her empty dress' (245) and held his breath in reverence at the scene. He eventually sings to her and half rouses her from her slumbers; but she sees a mortal man 'pallid chill and drear' (311) rather than the god who had sung to her through her slumbers. Provoked by her criticism, Porphyro is aroused 'Beyond a mortal man impassion'd far'. Here the poem hides a little in double entendre. Keats wanted to substitute a stanza which made it far clearer that consummation happened at this point but his publishers preferred his first version where Porphyro, 'Ethereal, flush'd and like a throbbing star' 'melted' 'Into her dream ... as the rose / Blendeth its odour with the violet / Solution sweet'. (318–22).

At this point the 'camera' (as it were) pans away discreetly to focus on the setting moon of St Agnes' Eve and the howling gale outside. Yet even here this plays a dramatic role in once again highlighting the contrast between the cold and hostile world outside of the relationship and the physical and emotional warmth and safety generated by these two young lovers. We enter their world so completely and yet know very little about their backgrounds beyond a few suggestive hints at a Montague-versus-Capulet type family feud. Such vagueness and the constant focus on each moment being described in all its sensual detail is all part of the universal appeal of the poem.

La belle dame sans merci

The song sung by the hopeful Porphyro is an interesting choice, as it was later taken up by Keats as the title of a much shorter poem on the subject of love. Originally the title of a medieval poem by Alain Chartier, 'La Belle Dame sans Merci' obviously falls into the provenance of a writer focusing on medieval courtly love – especially one who, even in the early stages of his bitter-sweet romance with Fanny Brawne, felt the harshness of love, its tempting quality away from his professed career, and the ever-present possibility of her changing her mind or being forced to do so by circumstance. More to the point, the beautiful lady without mercy might never accede to his impious desires.

If *The Eve of St Agnes* is Keats's dream love scenario, 'La belle dame sans merci' is his nightmare: that someone dedicated to his work (either as a knight or poet) could be distracted from that work by a beautiful but unreliable lady, one who eventually deserts him and leaves him to die a lonely and feverish death. A question he asks in a letter to Fanny

Brawne makes it clear that Keats knew how the knight felt: 'Ask yourself my love whether you are not very cruel to have so entrammelled me, so destroyed my freedom' (*Letters*, 263). Keats tells the tale in ballad form – highly suited not only to his medieval subject matter but also to the mood of unfinished business he wished to create, for the final line of each stanza is shorter than, often half as short as, the first three lines which each have the traditional eight syllables of a ballad. This has the double effect of drawing out the heavy negative syllables of such lines as 'And no birds sing' and leaving us, like the knight himself, expecting more only to be left with a sense of deficiency.

The poem begins with two questions given to the 'knight-at-arms' asking what can so 'ail' him as to be 'alone and palely loitering' by the side of a lake. The unspoken subtext is that he should be achieving great feats, in amongst society, performing acts of chivalry. Instead of this he is dallying, alone, passive, pale and sick. What could have caused this deviant behaviour? The knight's first answers are evasive: at best oblique, at worst misleading.

In fact Keats, characteristically, does not punctuate question and answer, so we are not sure where one stops and the other starts. The 'replies' such as they are, merely emphasize the time of year, with 'wither'd' undergrowth, squirrels prepared for winter and all birdsong ceased. In this barren landscape, the knight finds himself very much at home, with a 'lily on [his] brow' and the 'fading rose', the bloom of health 'fast withereth too' to be replaced by 'anguish moist and fever dew'. It seems that such inaction, such dallying around with beautiful women when there is a vocation to be pursued, might lead not merely to frustration but eventually the classic febrile symptoms of consumption which Keats had witnessed all too recently with the death of his brother Tom.

Being sick because of a heartless woman is of course a conventional courtly love theme – and one quite often used, as it is by Porphyro in *The Eve of St Agnes*, to persuade the lady to be kinder. Keats takes the convention to superb heights in his haunting ballad. The 'lady' whom the knight meets is a classic example of the femme fatale – but retains enough mystery about her to make us doubt her malicious intentions at all. As usual in Keats's romances, we are posed a series of unresolved questions:

* Is the lady a mortal, or, as the imagery used (by the knight) to describe her suggests, a 'faery's child'?

* Does she deliberately ensnare him or is he duped by his own weakness? After all it is he who 'set her on [his] pacing steed', chose to accompany her to 'her elfin grot' and 'shut her wild, wild eyes / With kisses four'.

* Are we to trust in his mysterious dream, with the awful warning from what seems like previous victims of the 'belle dame sans merci'?

Recent critics have emphasized that Keats's intentions seemed to undermine the fact that the knight is as much of a victim as he at first appears. In the only version published in Keats's lifetime, the manly 'knight-at-arms' is replaced by a 'wretched wight'; likewise the order of stanzas is changed around to emphasize the fact that the knight set her on his 'pacing steed'; and the belle dame is made more sympathetic, the sinister 'sidelong' with its connotations of sidling, being replaced by the more straightforward 'sideways' and she is given 'wild sad eyes' instead of 'wild wild eyes'. It seems that Keats was moving away from the simple binary divisions of victim and villain, and complicating both the motives of the characters and the responses of his readers.

Lamia

This was certainly the case in the last of his great poetic romances, written later in 1819. Again Keats portrays a femme fatale who dupes a hero before truth intervenes to leave him desolate. In this case the deception is not one of a 'faery's child' who merely deserts the unsuspecting male, but of a woman who is not really a woman at all.

She is a legendary creature taken from the world of Greek myth, half snake, half woman – a lamia. Keats found the story in a classically misanthropic English work, full of tales of misery and deception, Richard Burton's *Anatomy of Melancholy* – a work satirizing human folly, which Keats read avidly at this time, underlining particularly any episodes which highlighted the unreliability of women.

Keats embellished the original tale considerably, adding an introductory passage which partly balances out the misogyny of the whole. For here we meet Hermes, messenger of the gods who, in his desperation to discover the whereabouts of a coy nymph, grants Lamia a woman's shape. She is desperate to acquire this shape as she is enamoured of our blithely unaware hero, Lycius. Thus she trades the nymph's whereabouts for her own ends – and both male god and female Lamia are equally guilty of predatory behaviour, treating the objects of their lusts as commodities.

In the metamorphosis Lamia makes from being snake to woman we see a 'torture' and a sense of scale first encountered in the descriptions of the Titans in *Hyperion* with the 'volcanian' imagery prevalent.

Keats has chosen the heroic couplet here rather than the blank verse of the sonorous *Hyperion* or the static picturesque qualities of the stanza forms employed in *Isabella* or *The Eve*. The couplets give the verse a far brighter, blither feel than that achieved in the portentous *Hyperion*, an effect extended by one or two witty, distanced, almost Byronic touches in the poem. Keats's new 'experience of life' has enabled him to be very objective about his creations occasionally satirizing them – the fashionable Byronic 'manly' distancing, the tone of the experienced man-about-town – and even flashes of condoning the classic Byronic hero. At one point Lamia gives way to Lycius's masterful ways, and she 'lov'd the tyranny' (II, 81) as he becomes

> Perverse, with stronger fancy to reclaim
> Her wild and timid nature to his aim.

(II, 70–1)

t has been said that Lamia represents 'Keats's revised view of the poetic imagination'; 'her beauty is false and her effect on human life pernicious' (W. H. Evert, *Aesthetic and Myth in the Poetry of Keats*, 276–81). If this is the case then Keats's sudden mastery of various forms is an echo of his hero's mastery of the lamia. The heroic couplet is certainly a part of the effectiveness of the poem, with a new balanced control highlighted by his increased use of end-stopped self-contained couplets. However, unlike the Augustan poets, whose style he seems to borrow here, Keats is not afraid to use enjambment on occasions to break up the rhythm (such as 'now began/ To change'); nor even to have a triplet as opposed to a couplet ('drear', 'sear', 'tear') to emphasize the final line.

Lamia goes on, in her new guise as a 'full-born beauty new and exquisite' (172), to successfully entice Lycius into a relationship which is characterised by its blissful obliviousness to the outside world. They live in a little haven idyllic if isolated and stuffed full of all that the sensuous fancy can create. In fact, from the ugliness and pain of her metamorphosis Lamia has reinvented herself as a perfect male fantasy:

A virgin purest lipp'd, yet in the lore
Of love deep learned to the red heart's core

(189–90)

Eventually a philosopher who had formerly taught Lycius exposes Lamia as a mirage, a deceptive serpent rather than a pure beauty. Apollonius obviously stands for the hard truth of science and fact as opposed to the cosy world of fantasy. As the quotation from the critic Evert above attests, commentators have leapt upon this seeming emergence by the young Keats from his escapist tendency as a sign of a rejection of his youthful self. But this is to read the poem in a rather one-dimensional way. For, typically, Keats complicates the whole balance between truth and fantasy, often blaming Apollonius for his 'spiteful' 'cold philosophy' (II, 228, 230). The harsh ending where Lamia's exposure causes first her own disappearance and then the

death of Lycius is shown as brutal rather than mature – and the reader
is left uncertain which world is best, the factual or the fantastic.

ODES

Whilst Keats was working towards his epic, and composing romances
once every six months or so, he also produced countless shorter poems,
sonnets and lyrics. But in 1819 he took up the form of poetry which
has since been most associated with his name. The ode was a strange
choice in some ways, for it had been a favourite of the Augustans, poets
whom Keats had always defined himself against. However, with his
new-found technical poise (the assured control of Miltonic blank
verse, the stillness he created with the Spenserian stanza and even his
sudden expert use of the Augustan heroic couplet, in *Hyperion*, *The Eve*
and *Lamia* respectively) he seemed to be more open to different styles
but at the same time more confident that he could make these various
styles his own.

Ode to Psyche

The first of the spring odes to be composed,
'Ode to Psyche' indicates this new approach.
Keats commented that it was 'the first and only
[poem] with which I have taken even
moderate pains ... I think it reads the more
richly for it' (*Letters*, 253). These 'pains' are
seen in the complex rhyme-scheme Keats
constructed – partly based on his recent
experiments with the sonnet. He had claimed
in one sonnet, written about the sonnet form

KEYWORDS

Quatrain: a unit of verse
consisting of four lines,
generally with a self-
contained rhyme-scheme.

Octet: a unit of verse
consisting of eight lines,
generally with a self-
contained rhyme-scheme.

itself, that rhyme schemes should be more 'interwoven and complete'
to allow for an ongoing thought to be developed rather than cut off at
the end of each stanza or **quatrain** or **octet** ('If by dull rhymes our
English must be chained' [5]). Thus the first stanza of the ode begins
with a regular alternate rhyme-scheme but then becomes quite
random, making us wait sometimes for a rhyme which never comes,
with unrhymed lines such as lines 10 and 14.

This gives a freshness and spontaneity as well as a sense of the renewed harmony and rightness by the end of each stanza which returns to the alternate rhyme-scheme of the beginning. Together with the use of occasional shorter lines for effect (for instance the dramatic answer to the question at the end of the first stanza, identifying the goddess), these innovations are controlled, and technically very accomplished, and yet have the feeling of artless novelty about them.

Such a bid for freedom within the old forms is exactly right for his subject matter here, as Keats takes a traditional subject for an ode, a classical goddess, but gives it a very modern treatment. For he chooses a goddess who was invented after the times when the ancient gods were formally worshiped – and his stated aim in the poem is to right this wrong. In an elevated style, typical of the ode in that he directly addresses the goddess, he claims 'I will be thy priest'. But in a departure from all formal types of religious ceremony, the 'fane' or temple he will build, will be

> In some untrodden region of my mind,
> Where branched thoughts, new grown with pleasant pain,
> Instead of pines shall murmur in the wind:
>
> And in the midst of this wide quietness
> A rosy sanctuary will I dress
> With the wreath'd trellis of a working brain
> With buds, and bells, and stars without a name,
> With all the gardener Fancy e'er could feign,
> Who breeding flowers, will never breed the same
>
> (50–63)

Thus what had seemed a slight poem, almost playfully referring to ancient gods, has become a serious vision of the imaginative and creative process. And vision is exactly the right word to choose, for the poem had begun with Keats claiming that he had 'seen' Psyche and her fabled lover, Cupid, embracing in the woods just as the ancients claimed to have seen the gods in the landscape around them. A self-consciously

ridiculous dream has become something far more profound. For
Psyche was supposed to be a personification of the human soul and the
word is now more commonly used for the mind.

Keats uses her as a means of expressing his view that the creative
process involved in being human entails an exploration of 'untrodden
region[s] of [the] mind', what today we would term the unconscious.
It also means engaging with that typically Keatsian oxymoron of
'pleasant pain' – the joys and sorrows of life felt to the full; and it means
creating one's own mental landscape, using the Fancy or imagination
to transmogrify all that you encounter into a garden, a 'rosy sanctuary'
individual to you, because only you have experienced your own specific
circumstances.

Just as the rhyme-scheme returns to the beginning, so Keats turns back
to his goddess at the end, claiming that the 'sanctuary' he has created
will be an ideal place for Psyche:

> And there shall be for thee all soft delight
> That shadowy thought can win,
> A bright torch, and a casement ope at night,
> To let the warm love in!
>
> (64–7)

Once again 'shadowy' rather than clear-cut and dogmatic 'thought' is
presented as the ideal. The last lines refer to the myth that Cupid would
only continue visiting Psyche (which he effected through her window
each night) as long as she refrained from looking at him or lighting a
torch. It seems that, according to Keats's view, the 'bright torch' is
necessary to examine the 'shadowy' places of the mind; but more
important perhaps is the welcome one affords to 'the warm love' of
human contact and relationships. Ultimately, it is by involvement and
commitment and love that we people and enrich our inner landscape.

Ode to a Nightingale

We cannot be sure which of the odes Keats composed next but it is
generally assumed that the 'Ode to a Nightingale' follows on from the

'Ode to Psyche'. As in all the odes, Keats addresses an artefact or a personification, or in this case a bird, directly. However, there is far more of a sense of personal involvement, almost confession in the 'Ode to a Nightingale' with the song of the bird generally a backdrop to the poet's own emotions and cropping up every now and then like a refrain – or like the elaborate rhyme-schemes which Keats further refined for this ode. The 'Ode to a Nightingale' swoops and soars through moods of ecstasy and despair as the poet meditates and deliberates on the transience and pain of human existence.

The poem opens by trying to account for the 'drowsy numbness' which paradoxically 'pains' the poet as he seems to be slipping towards the forgetfulness of the mythical river 'Lethe'. He refers to opiates, wine, the fierce power of envy and the artistic heights of the bird itself as a series of possible reasons for this sense of being at one remove from the hurly burly of life; but eventually settles on an unusual explanation: 'being too happy in thine happiness' (6) – the power, so prized by Keats, of empathy. Here the intensifier 'too' indicates the poet's awareness that even empathy, the instinct which connects us most nearly with our fellow humans, can be a form of escapism.

In a letter to Shelley written over a year later, Keats was to state his view that an artist 'must have "self concentration" selfishness perhaps' and advised the older poet to 'curb [his] magnanimity and be more of an artist, and "load every rift" of [his] subject with ore' (Letters, 390). It seems that he wavered between a view of the imagination as a selfless act of empathy with other characters, almost an obliteration of self, and that kind of psychological self-examination which Wordsworth had made his own provenance. This debate lies at the heart of contemporaneous literary theory. Either way Keats always felt that each chosen subject should be crammed full of the golden 'ore' of poetic invention and expression which he had found in 'realms of gold' of the great poets of the past and which he hoped to replicate himself.

'Ode to a Nightingale' certainly has some examples of such 'ore'. A high proportion of the 80 lines of the poem make it into any good book of quotations. Apart from the sheer word-magic, what makes such phrases as 'the viewless wings of Poesy' quite so memorable is the pattern Keats creates, as he did in *The Eve of St Agnes*, of a binary division, despairing world against ecstatic haven. In this case the despairing world is starkly described as a place 'Where youth grows pale, and spectre-thin, and dies' – a world Keats knew all too well as his own young brother, Tom, had died less than six months before. The haven created by association with the bird's song (a song which, Keats notes, has not changed for centuries) is a place which one can enter via the poetic imagination, a place full of a 'tender' moonlight, the scent of 'hawthorn and the pastoral eglantine',

KEYWORD

Onomatopoeic: words where the sound echoes the meaning, e.g. twitter, cuckoo, or (less obviously) murmur.

> And mid-May's eldest child,
> The coming musk-rose, full of dewy wine,
> The murmurous haunt of flies on summer eves.

                                                                              (48–50)

Even the famously **onomatopoeic** final line contributes to the beauty of the scene as child-like associations are prevalent here, just as 'the

Queen-Moon' lends a maternal overseeing presence to this bower of motherly safety. In an ecstasy of comfort the poet feels that

> Now more than ever seems it rich to die,
> To cease upon the midnight with no pain

(55–6)

Thus death is the ultimate escape towards the Lethe of forgetfulness. But it is at this point that the poet is brought back to his 'sole self' out of his visionary haven. He turns on the fancy, calling his imagination a 'deceiving elf', for not proving a reliable refuge from the world of pain, merely a temporary and fleeting escape. But the poem is typically left unresolved as the poet then questions which is the 'real' reality – the world he has woken up to with its pain and fears, or the intensely realised 'vision' he has experienced so fully: 'Fled is that music: – Do I wake or sleep?' (80).

Ode on a Grecian Urn

Like the 'Ode to a Nightingale', the 'Ode on a Grecian Urn' is a meditation on immortality – this time not in the guise of changeless birdsong, but great art. An urn is a jar often used to contain the ashes of a dead person and in ancient Greek civilization these urns were highly decorated artefacts, many of which have survived to this day.

There is a paradoxical deathless quality to a relic made for a person so long since dead. In fact the whole civilization which produced the urn has passed away and this provides Keats with the beginnings of his contemplation on the urn. For while the pictures on the urn tell a story, we cannot know exactly what the story is – but can appreciate their beauty simply as beauty. We do not know and cannot ask 'What leaf-fring'd legend haunts about [the urn's] shape' – whether the figures presented are 'men or gods'. Or rather we *can* ask (as Keats proves in a series of rhetorical questions addressed directly to the silent urn) but there will be no definitive reply.

More paradoxes are found in the 'action' Keats finds on what is essentially a static piece of art – as if a moment of great drama has been frozen eternally. For a 'Bold Lover' is about to kiss his sweetheart whilst pipers play in a Dionysian 'wild ecstasy' of music and dance, 'pursuit' and 'struggle to escape' (9–10). Keats finds the fact that the music can be heard only in the imagination an advantage, for 'Heard melodies are sweet, but those unheard/ Are sweeter' (11–12). Keats is perhaps suggesting that a work of art which gives us space to employ our own creative processes is greater than those which didactically or descriptively pin us down.

The same is true, according to this theory, and according to Keats's practice, of narrative. A narrative which lets us work things out for ourselves gives us more imaginative space than one of neatly tied up ends (and we think back to the vagueness of the disappearing lovers in *The Eve*, the unresolved predicament of the knight in 'La belle dame' and the strange disappearance of Lamia). In this case, the 'Bold Lover' will never know the outcome of the embrace he seems about to enjoy – a predicament which fascinates the observing poet, giving him room to meditate not merely upon narrative, but upon the nature of art and more generally on the whole human predicament. For the lover, trapped statically and awaiting fulfilment, is first pitied for his situation. But then Keats changes tack and congratulates this man for he has everything to anticipate and nothing to regret, as he permanently contemplates a lover

> [who] cannot fade, though thou hast not thy bliss,
> For ever wilt thou love, and she be fair

(19–20)

Being outside time has its advantages, Keats concludes, with a bitter look at the fading beauty of real women, the doom to which all our relationships and all our lives are inexorably leading. The world of art is different, for the leaves on the urn will never drop their leaves, the lovers will never tire or their passions fade.

The fourth stanza looks at a fresh part of the urn's decorative tale – with a fresh perspective on the same issue. Static anticipated *pleasure* may be all very well, Keats implies, but what about static anticipated doom? What about the 'heifer' who is being led to the 'sacrifice'? And, for that matter, what about the 'little town' pictured in the distance for ever 'emptied of ... folk', for ever 'desolate'? Just as with the 'Ode to a Nightingale', Keats wavers between positive pictures of the joys of escaping into timeless art, and the negative qualities associated with such a distraction from the pain of a transitory life.

This unresolved stance weaves its way through the famous final stanza of the poem. Viewed in one sense, the urn is a 'Fair attitude' – a beautiful, poised and distanced pose who advises us like a 'friend' that 'beauty is truth, truth beauty'. Viewed in another sense, the urn is a 'Cold Pastoral' whose bucolic beauty, whilst it may not fade, cannot fully enter into the warmth and spirit of what it is to be human. For part of the whole 'truth' involved in humanity, as Keats's next great ode reminds us, is an appreciation of the darker aspects of our lives – only to find great 'beauty' even there.

Ode on Melancholy

In this ode the knowledge that 'Beauty ... must die' (21) is not to be forgotten but viewed instead as the essence of life, heightening our appreciation rather than causing us to turn elsewhere. The whole poem is a warning against the 'Lethe' of forgetfulness, the kind of blinkered, havened view of the world Keats had explored in the preceding odes, the extreme escape from self whether in art or nature. Here he advises us against the kind of Gothic melancholy which had become quite fashionable at his time but which has always formed a strand of society – a type of adolescent wallowing in life-denying gloom. Thus there are two extremes to be avoided – the joyous escapism which sees no pain in life; and a type of false melancholy which cannot appreciate the full beauty because it is so focused on darkness and death.

The first stanza is one long rejection of the almost religious worship of this dark side – with its imagery of poison ('Wolf's-bane', deadly nightshade, yew-berries counted like the beadsman's rosary beads from *The Eve of St Agnes*) and death (the deathwatch beetle, the nocturnal owl or a 'death-moth' worshipped instead of the goddess Psyche – who was normally symbolized by a far more life-affirming butterfly). The reason given recalls in both sentiment and phrasing the beginning of *Hyperion*, where Saturn wallows in inactive misery, seemingly one step away from the insentient trees which enshroud his misery, like 'shade on shade'. For if you turn this way, warns Keats, then

> shade to shade will come too drowsily,
> And drown the wakeful anguish of the soul.

(9–10)

Just as in the 'Ode to a Nightingale', the intensifier 'too' is all-important. But whereas in the earlier ode Keats had worried about being 'too happy' in his escape with the nightingale's song, here he worries about too much wallowing in self-indulgence, which makes one unaware of the outside world at all. Be alive to the 'anguish' of this transitory world he advises. Neither in a going out of one's spirit, nor in a completely inward concentration on one's own pain is the true melancholy to be found – but in a fully observant wakefulness, remaining alive to the beauty and the sad truths of pain and transience.

The images of beauty catalogued in the second stanza, images upon which one should 'glut thy sorrow', are all characterized either by their fleeting quality (a rainbow, a cloud, a mood) or by their dark associations – whilst the cloud may foster spring flowers, it 'hides the green hill in an April shroud'; the mood described in the mistress is anger and her hand is 'Emprison[ed]'; even the reviving flowers are 'droop-headed' because of the rain. So at the selfsame time as the wakeful poet notices the beauty, he intertwines it with images of sadness. At the same time he intersperses in the stanza the quality which he associated with growth of spirit in what he termed the 'vale of Soul-making' (*Letters*, 249). For the soul grows, 'gluts', 'feed[s]' upon the 'rich' experiences of life, whether seemingly negative or simply beautiful. This, according to the poet, is what gives us our identity.

The third and final stanza foresees the poet's own death as a sacrifice to a goddess-like figure of Melancholy, whose 'sovran shrine' is in direct contrast to the false worship of gothic gloom described at the beginning of the poem. The *real* Melancholy is characterized by a heightened awareness, an extreme sensitivity to the intensity of life associated with the artist at his greatest. For her 'shrine' is

> seen of none save him whose strenuous tongue
> Can burst Joy's grape against his palate fine

(27–8).

This is about the ultimate connoisseur – not merely of fine wine, but of the fineness of life itself, in a full appreciation of all its passing glories.

To Autumn

Keats's final great ode also concerns the transitory, the passing. This is fitting not merely because he was contemplating the end of a season the end of the year, but because of what that year (1819) had contained – and what was to come in the next. Only 12 months earlier his brother Tom had lain mortally ill. Out of this pain, and out of his appreciation for the beauty of his new relationship with Fanny, Keats had been more inspired than ever. The coming winter, however, was to be the last flourish of creativity before he discovered that he too would die of consumption. A heightened awareness of the beauty of the passing season seems a portent of the end. And yet the mood of the poem is one of calm acceptance.

With 'Ode to a Nightingale', this is perhaps the most accomplished of his briefer poems. But despite the shared subject matter of English (as opposed to classical) natural scenery, the poems are quite different. Whereas 'Nightingale' is characterized by the exploratory urgency of its tone, 'To Autumn' has a 'mellow', assured, almost resigned air. The spring ode is full of questions, but the only questions in 'To Autumn' concern 'the songs of spring', to which he quickly replies 'think not of them' – as if the poet is aware of the uncertainty of his spring odes and is now beyond their insistent questing.

Keats was inspired by some late clement weather towards the end of September whilst he was staying in Winchester, working on his revised version of *Hyperion*. He notes the creativity of nature and mankind at this last flourish of sunshine, with bees and farmers, orchard-workers and gleaners, working to get their harvests in. But the pace of the poem is slow not urgent, with the bees thinking 'that warm days will never cease', farmworkers 'sitting careless', 'Drows'd' and 'patient' (10, 13, 17, 21). Even the stanza length is stretched out from the ten lines of the 'Ode on Melancholy' to 11, as if the season is elongated in its effort to cram all the goodness of life in. The poem is characterized by a full ripeness, energetic without haste, aware without wallowing in the grief of transience. It is justly one of the most famous and beloved in the language.

The season is personified and addressed directly in the poem as the guiding spirit, the goddess behind all this abundance and creativity. She is pictured first as 'conspiring' with the 'maturing sun' (2–3) to produce all the archetypal crops of an English autumn (vines, apples, hazel nuts, flowers, corn); and then in the second stanza she is seen in various vignettes in the guise of the agricultural workers of the time: in a granary; harvesting in the fields with a sickle or scythe; as a gleaner collecting the left-over ears of corn in a basket; or overseeing the conversion of the apples to cider at the 'cyder-press' (21). For just as the bees must preserve their nectar over the lean months of winter, so the goodness of nature's apples must be compressed, conserved to be appreciated for much longer.

The parallel with Keats's early work, *Endymion*, as well as the 'Ode on Melancholy' is perhaps significant. For it is as if Keats himself is storing up these images, these 'Thing[s] of beauty' to be a 'joy forever' in the timeless sweetness of great art. Apart from the greater maturity in style, what makes this such an advance on *Endymion*, is its appreciation not merely of the joy but the melancholy.

The suggestions of such melancholy are faint at first. However, in the final stanza they are made more palpable. Yet even here they are mitigated by their inherent beauty. The day is 'soft-dying', in a stunningly described sunset; 'in a wailful choir the small gnats mourn … borne aloft/ As the light wind lives or dies'; the 'full-grown lambs' are ready for slaughter; 'Hedge-crickets' may 'sing' but it will be a swan-song; and swallows gather to depart. Nothing may escape the inexorable approach of the unmentioned winter. And yet even here Keats gives us hope: a 'red-breast whistles' providing a little counterpoint to the beautiful but melancholy, truthful but softly described, 'wailful choir'.

✳ ✳ ✳ *SUMMARY* ✳ ✳ ✳

- Keats's output shows a rapidly maturing talent honed by love and pain.

- Many of his lines have become part of the language.

6 Themes and theories

LETTERS

Without writing a 'Defence of Poetry' a *Biographia Literaria* or even a brilliant preface to his published poetry (as did Shelley, Coleridge and Wordsworth respectively), Keats remains among the most quoted and respected literary theorists of the Romantic Age. Instead of the formal essay on poetry, Keats has left us his letters – a storehouse of wisdom and wit which his friends and relations treasured, kept and eventually submitted to the first biographers of the poet some years after his death. Amongst all the news and gossip, anecdote and angst (which all help form our view of the poet at work), there are also scraps of poems quoted and, most fascinating of all, Keats's views on life and literature.

More recently, one of the most respected (and demanding) of critics, T. S. Eliot, claimed that 'There is hardly one statement of Keats about poetry, which, when considered carefully and with due allowance for the difficulties of communication, will not be found to be true: and what is more, true for a greater and more mature poetry than anything Keats ever wrote' (T. S. Eliot, *The Use of Poetry and the Use of Criticism*, Harvard University Press, 1933, 101). These 'statements ... about poetry' as well as forming a part of possibly the most readable correspondence of an English literary figure, are certainly a useful starting point for an examination of the poet's own work.

NEGATIVE CAPABILITY

One of the first and most famous of Keats's pronouncements on literature is one that should stand as a warning to us when considering either Keats's poetry or the theory behind that poetry. For Keats cautions against being too dogmatic, too systematic – but always to allow room for doubt, for questions. In a letter written in November 1817 to his brothers, he discussed that quality 'which Shakespeare possessed so enormously – I mean *Negative Capability*, that is when man is capable of being in uncertainties, Mysteries, doubts, without any irritable reaching after fact & reason' (*Letters*, 370). In other words, this type of creative mind can make a positive strength out of doubt; it opposes the definite and the dogmatic in favour of paradox and uncertainty.

We do as well to remember this when we examine Keats's pronouncements; like many human statements, they are not exercises in mere logic, but can be contradicted or viewed in another light, often in the same paragraph, stanza or even sentence. Literature, and indeed, the whole human condition, Keats seems to be saying, is too complex to be reduced to simplistic and sweeping judgements.

Later Keats expressed the same sentiment slightly differently: 'The only means of strengthening one's intellect is to make up one's mind about nothing – to let the mind be a thoroughfare for all thoughts. Not a select party' (*Letters*, 326). This belief was given in an age which was becoming far more definite in its views, particularly in the areas of politics and morality. After the latitudinarianism of *laissez-faire* eighteenth-century religion, the French Revolution had hardened and polarized views in Britain. Most of Keats's friends were of the liberal and radical anti-establishment faction and, indeed, Keats claimed that he wished to contribute in some meaningful way to 'the liberal side of the question'. But he came to believe that the greatest poetry should be far more than simplistic party-aligned dogma. Literature, and life, are far more complex than that.

Likewise, Keats is rarely strident in his poetry, believing that 'Man should not dispute or assert but whisper results to his neighbour' and disapproving of 'poetry which has a palpable design upon us' (*Letters*, 66, 61). He later criticized Shelley for favouring art which had an overt didactic 'purpose' – always trying to support a cause or prove a case. Keats's own poetry retains much of its richness through a refusal to condemn or condone simply. There are very few examples of outright evil in his work. Many of his characters are misguided or foolish; many are devious or insensitive. But few are simplistically either good or evil. In fact, Keats reserves most opprobrium for a character who is, according to the strict schemata of the poem, a good man. In *Lamia*, Apollonius (the wise sage who condemns Lycius' young bride, identifying her as a serpent) is so dogmatic in his wisdom that he actually destroys Lycius. His is the stance identified with contemporary science ('Cold philosophy') which cannot conceive of any good coming out of deception, or fancy. Such a view would 'Conquer all mysteries by rule and line', 'unweave a rainbow' and leave no room for the magical uncertainties of life (*Lamia*, II, 230–8).

Thus, much of Keats's work involves questions without necessarily providing ready-made answers. As he put it, 'A Question is the best beacon towards a little Speculation' (*Letters*, 32) – a maxim best exemplified in the great spring odes of 1819. To pin him down to a particular view of life, or the treatment of a theme, is difficult. It is not so much that he lacks consistency as that he is continually looking at fresh angles on topics as diverse as gender and power, the ideal and the real. Thus his rich and often ambiguous poetic style is matched by an ambivalent attitude.

EMPATHY AND IDENTITY

It became fashionable amongst Romantic critics and writers to separate authors into one of two types: those who focused on their own personality, in what Keats referred to as the 'wordsworthian or egotistical sublime' (*Letters*, 157); and those who, like Shakespeare, poured all their creative energies and empathies into the characters and situations they created. Typically for Keats, he remained negatively capable on these two stances.

He seems at first sight to belong very much to Shakespeare's kind, pronouncing that 'Men of Genius ... have not any individuality, any determined Character.' In the same letter he observed of himself that 'if a Sparrow come before my Window I take part in its existince [sic] and pick about the Gravel' (*Letters*, 36, 38). He admired the fact that the Bard 'has as much delight in conceiving an Iago as an Imogen' (*Letters*, 157) – in other words evil and good characters are equally enjoyable to create. The poet's own identity is lost in his empathies with the characters of his creation, whether good or evil.

Perhaps this is best illustrated in *The Eve of St Agnes* where Keats 'has as much delight' in painting the scheming and predatory Porphyro as the dreamily innocent Madeline. The poet throws himself into both characters and their intensely imagined situations and points of view – whether it is Madeline's hopeful absorption as she prepares for her supernatural vision, or Porphyro's amazed delight as he watches from the vantage point of the closet. By the choice of such minute details as the 'soft and chilly nest' in which Madeline lies, and the watchful Porphyro, almost too afraid to breathe lest he wake her, we the readers are made to feel not merely present, but partaking of the situation from two points of view.

However, later, despite his ambition that he might one day write 'a few fine plays' (*Letters*, 341), he came to believe that an artist 'must have "self concentration" selfishness perhaps'. Likewise he often expressed the view that Wordsworth was the greatest living writer, largely because of his knowledge of the human heart – a knowledge which he largely explored in an inward examination rather than through Shakespearian empathy (*Letters*, 93). This self-exploration is often apparent in the spring odes with their concentration on inner feelings and use of the first person.

WOMEN AND LOVE

One of the reasons Keats was pilloried in his own time was in his lax attitude to morals. A new prudery had begun to prevail: this was both a reaction to the perceived licentiousness associated with the French Revolution and its liberal supporters, and a response to the increased readership of women and the lower classes – groups of people who had to be (patronizingly) 'protected' from vulgar immorality posing as poetry.

By including all the nymphs and dusky maidens in his poetry, Keats was unashamedly placing himself with the liberals. The epigraph he chose for his first volume of verse shows his awareness of the link between 'delight' and 'liberty' – libertarian morals to accompany more liberal politics. The settings of his poems, whether medieval and full of superstition and courtly love, or classical with goddesses and grecian nakedness, form a mode of discourse where presentation of sex was more possible than outright representations of lust in a modern context. But conservative critics saw through the thin disguise and condemned the poet for his lack of 'the regulating principle of religion' (Josiah Conder in the *Eclectic Review*, September 1820). These reviews did not merely concern such early verse as the infamous reference to nymphs in 'Sleep and Poetry' (where Keats promises to 'Play with their fingers, touch their shoulders white/ Into a pretty shrinking with a bite / As hard as lips can make it' [107–9]; it also refers to the later more mature poetry (such as the celebrations of 'warm love' in the 'Ode to Psyche' and the 'Ode on a Grecian Urn').

Expressions of physical love were, according to Keats, not just 'the mere commingling of passionate breath' but an expression of the very life-blood of the universe (*Endymion*, I, 833). He often gave sex a reverential, almost mystical quality, as in the 'Ode to Psyche' or the 'Ode on Melancholy' where it helps give access to those 'untrodden regions of [the] mind' so necessary for creativity; or in *Lamia* where intimacy creates a fantastical state, a haven from the pressures of society; or in *The Eve* where Porphyro, 'Beyond a mortal man impassion'd far ... Ethereal, flush'd, and like a throbbing star', takes on a god-like status whilst making love to Madeline. At other times passion is described as a fleeting and therefore torturing pleasure ('Ode on a Grecian Urn'). But generally, as befits this poet of adolescence, sex is idealized – and occasionally graphically physical.

The lives and loves of the characters in his poetry occasionally project his own idiosyncratic fears and anxieties as well as his joys. For every eulogy on love there is an angst-laden fearful tale of betrayal and deceit. Many of these anxious poems have been attributed to his own lack of security from an early age. In a letter to Fanny Brawne, he claimed that he had 'never known any unalloy'd happiness for many days together: the death of sickness of some one has always spoilt my hours' (*Letters*, 263). As one of his biographers puts it, discussing his mother's 'disappearance and subsequent disgrace', 'The idealized woman of his crucial early experience, beautiful and recklessly affectionate, had betrayed and abandoned him in a manner beyond his understanding, and forever afterward he was haunted by the fear that any woman he loved should play him false and then leave him' (Aileen Ward, *John Keats: The Making of a Poet*, Secker and Warburg, 1963).

Late in his career Keats realized that 'there is a tendency to class women in my books with roses and sweetmeats, – they never see themselves dominant' (*Letters*, 391). Certainly women are often merely the objects of desire and pleasure in the early verse. But in his later work, Keats often reversed and occasionally actually critiqued such attitudes. In *Lamia* the god Hermes is mocked for such a wanton selfishness; and Lamia herself displays a similarly predatory attitude to the male god as they exchange methods for ensnaring their respective victims. Clearly women, in the world Keats portrays, can be the sexual predators as often as the victims. The 'belle dame sans merci' for instance is 'dominant' to the extent of being not merely a femme fatale, but a serial destroyer of masculine pretension (the 'kings and princes too' are reduced to 'pale' shadows of their former selves, 'in thrall' to this bewitching creature). Thus Keats undermines many of the contemporary patriarchal views which assumed that women were always passive, must be protected and were sweet and innocent victims. Far from being sweet, the *belle dame* is *sans merci* – lacking, or at least using for her own ends, the nurturing aspect of women which convention would have us expect.

The whole issue of male–female relations can become a metaphor for other power structures in Keats's work, largely because of his use of mythology. By focusing on the world of the gods Keats gives his tales a universal, archetypal quality. Thus Endymion's search for his goddess becomes the adolescent's search for the goal of self-realization; the dark maternal presences in *Hyperion* are perhaps expressions of a deep-seated male angst about female power as Saturn is seen bowed as if 'list'ning to the Earth / His ancient mother for some comfort yet' (20–1). These relations between powerless and powerful, so naturally drawn from childhood experiences common to all of us, can also be seen as applying to the political processes of the time. There is a continual interplay of passive and active roles in Keats's depictions of the relations between the sexes – and the roles, as we have seen, are not always those traditionally proscribed by tradition. Perhaps Keats is voicing the concerns of a marginalized group (his own social status was continually mocked in his own day) and positing the possibility of an exchange of roles in a larger sense.

DREAMS AND THE IDEAL

It is scarcely surprising that with a life as insecure and full of pain as Keats's he should turn to literature for an escape, throwing himself into both his reading and writing with an intensity born of anguish. And his poetry self-consciously creates an imaginary dreamworld full of pleasures denied to him through lack of opportunity.

Whether these dreamscapes flesh out an adolescent fantasy, or embody solid middle-class aspirations has long been a cause of speculation. Certainly Byron thought that Keats's imagination was a little overwrought, full of substitutes for real women: he condemned Keats's work as 'a sort of mental masturbation – frigging his *Imagination*' rather than looking squarely at a real world which he had experienced as fully as Byron and his ilk.

Keats acknowledged this quality in himself in the preface to *Endymion*: 'The imagination of a boy is healthy, and the mature imagination of a man is healthy; but there is a space of life between, in which the soul is in a ferment, the character undecided, the way of life uncertain, the ambition thick-sighted: thence proceeds mawkishness ...' It is in his exploration of this 'space of life' that Keats has been marked as a pioneer in his work by such critics as John Bayley, Christopher Ricks and Marjorie Levinson. The title of Ricks's book, *Keats and Embarrassment*, sums up the views of these critics who note how it is the cringeworthy and crass 'badness' of Keats's style (especially in his early work) that his exploration of life is at its most interesting. For in moments of extraordinary honesty, and seeming to lack the self-consciousness of most poets, Keats displays all the embarrassing hallmarks of what today we would term a teenager.

Keats seems at times simultaneously aware of strategies for acquiring imaginatively what he cannot have in reality, and unselfconscious in the expression of them. In the early work, 'Sleep and Poetry', he describes the nymph-filled sleepy world full of comfort and luxury that he would explore in his early verse. In his more mature work, he claims, he will aspire to describe the 'nobler life,/ Where I may find the agonies, the strife/ Of human hearts'.

This self-conscious boundary between juvenile luxuriousness and mature nobility is made less distinct when he describes these 'visions' of his future poetical career suddenly vanishing. He is brought suddenly and lamentably back to the here and now: 'A sense of real things comes doubly strong,/ And, like a muddy stream, would bear along/ My soul to nothingness.' ('Sleep and Poetry', 96–7, 123–5, 155–9). It is clear that even 'the agonies, the strife/ Of human hearts' which he would explore in his mature work has at best a tangential relationship with the 'muddy stream' of life. Poetry, for Keats, should not hold up a mirror to life but explore alternatives to it. Whilst 'agonies' have their place in these fantasy worlds, situations are always characterized by their dreamy otherness. As he put it when contrasting a more realistic contemporary poetry, '[Byron] describes what he sees – I describe what I imagine – Mine is the hardest task' (*Letters*, 314).

Often his poems do not merely exemplify this theory and describe enchanted worlds of mythology or the 'faery lands forlorn' he explores in the 'Ode to a Nightingale'. They are not just set in these worlds but are about the whole subject of escapist worlds per se. The 'Ode to a Nightingale' chiefly concerns the poet's flight to an imaginary world full of the 'starry Fays' (or fairies) of fantasy – away from the 'weariness, the fever, and the fret' of real life (37, 23); *Lamia* is all about the creative processes of inventing a luxurious haven away from the harsh truths of society; as he phrased it in a poem all about the escapist powers of the imagination, 'Ever let the Fancy roam,/Pleasure never is at home' ('Fancy', 1–2).

At other times, he went further in his claims for the imagination – which he felt could be more than a mere escapist balm. As he phrased it in an early letter, 'The Imagination may be compared to Adam's dream – he awoke and found it truth' (*Letters*, 37). In other words, one's imagination may be the means by which one effects change. The dream (in this case Adam's dream of his future partner Eve as described in Milton's *Paradise Lost*) can, if experienced intensely enough, become reality. The whole of *Endymion* is about such self-fulfilling prophecies with the hero eventually actualizing the dream he has had – and finding his ideal goddess. A better-known example comes from *The Eve of St Agnes* where Madeline's dreams of a future lover become palpable.

Typically, Keats was deeply ambivalent about the status of the dream worlds he was so apt to create. Is Lamia's 'purple-lined palace of sweet sin' (*Lamia* II, 31) ultimately a positive creation, or a 'foul dream' as Apollonius describes it (*Lamia* II, 271)? Is the timeless world of the 'Ode on a Grecian Urn' a 'Cold Pastoral' or a beautiful truth? The Urn would have us believe that a transient life should always be avoided by escaping into the dreamy world of art; conversely, Apollonius deems all such escapes a pernicious evasion of the one true factual world. It is interesting that both these extreme positions are given the same adjective: the urn is a 'Cold Pastoral' too removed from life to retain any of its real warmth; whilst Apollonius is roundly condemned for his 'Cold Philosophy' which cannot allow for the very real and human need for dreams. Only the negatively capable can see the benefits and the dangers of the dreamworld. Like Lamia, Keats responds to a painful life by creating these worlds and 'set[s] [him]self, high-thoughted, how to dress / The misery in fit magnificence' (II, 115–16); unlike her, he is fully aware, and takes into his creation elements of a world of pain and suffering.

BEAUTY AND INTENSITY

In a letter to his brother, Keats described *Lamia* in terms which clarify his ideals for poetry and his opinion of contemporary literary taste: 'there is that sort of fire in it which must take hold of people in some way – give them either pleasant or unpleasant sensation. What they want is a sensation of some sort' (*Letters*, 308). Other statements made in the letters at various points in his writing career further develop this theory:

✳ 'I have the same Idea of all our Passions as of Love they are all in their sublime, creative of essential Beauty' (*Letters*, 37).

✳ 'The excellence of every Art is its intensity, capable of making all disagreeables evaporate, from their being in close relationship with Beauty and truth' (*Letters*, 42).

✳ 'I think poetry should surprise by a fine excess and not by Singularity' (*Letters*, 69).

✳ 'with a great poet the sense of Beauty overcomes every other consideration, or rather obliterates all consideration' (*Letters*, 43).

Intensity and beauty are the hallmarks of a Keats poem, the 'fine excess' of his imaginary worlds characterized by a plenitude of imagined sensations. He makes clear that 'all our Passions' 'pleasant or unpleasant', if presented in a sensational manner, become not merely an interesting subject for poetry, but are 'creative of essential beauty'. Thus we are given the sad stories of *Isabella*, or the knight-at-arms in 'La belle dame sans merci', where the pathos and desolation is not an ugly sensation but is 'sweetly sad'. In tone, in execution, in style, in rhythm, these potentially alarming subjects are made beautiful.

It is not merely intense emotions but intense physical sensation that are typically Keatsian characteristics. His friend and mentor, Charles Cowden Clarke, recorded how Keats would throw himself physically into the reading of a poem: 'He hoisted himself up, and looked burly and dominant, as he said, "what an image that is – *sea-shouldering whales!*"' (Charles and Mary Cowden Clarke, *Recollections of Writers* 1878, ed. Robert Gittings, Fontwell, 126). Such physicality was certainly an ideal when he went on to write his own poetry.

This intensity is not only a characteristic of Keats's poetry but often its subject. Thus the 'Ode on Melancholy' is about finding beauty in the saddest moments; and likewise recognizing the sadness inherent in all beauty. But it is more than this: it is about searching for the most extreme, the most intense experiences and emotions, to find them and feast upon them in a concentrated effort to extract all the beauty one can from life. From the 'sorrow' inherent in a 'morning rose' (is this archetypal symbol of beauty sad by association or because it is transient?) to the 'rich anger' of one's 'mistress' – beauty and sad truth are inseparable. For just as beauty cannot be created without a knowledge that it must die, so there is no moment so sad that it cannot be transmuted into beautiful art: as the Urn puts it, '"Beauty is truth, truth beauty," – that is all/ Ye know on earth, and all ye need to know' ('Ode on a Grecian Urn', 49–50).

Perhaps Keatsian intensity is best exemplified in the second stanza of the 'Ode to a Nightingale' where sensuous experience is distilled to its very quintessence. The poet wishes for relief from his confused emotions, but rather than merely describing a glass of wine, he cries:

> O for a draught of vintage! that hath been
> Cool'd a long age in the deep-delv'd earth,
> Tasting of Flora and the country green,
> Dance, and Provencal song, and sunburnt mirth!
> O for a beaker full of the warm South ...

> (11–15)

Here the coolness contrasts with the world of 'fever and fret' Keats is trying to evade and the alliterative 'deep-delv'd' reminds us not merely of cellars but the hands that have created them; we are led by association with 'earth' into a consideration of the vegetation (of which Flora is the classical goddess) and the local music and dance and merriment – all this brought to life in one glass of wine which is not even present but merely wished for! This is the type of intensity Keats meant – a mixture of strong passions and sensitive expression of them. This is a vision of longing 'seen of none save him whose strenuous tongue/ Can burst Joy's grape against his palate fine' ('Ode on Melancholy', 27–8).

When he advised Shelley to 'load every rift of [his] subject with ore' (*Letters*, 390), it was a poetry as full of meaning as this that he had in mind – one where each object brings with it a plethora of associations and a dense richness of meaning. Poetry should create such an intensity of sensation and emotion, that its 'fine excess' should overwhelm the reader – just as the wine can condense the essence of a whole country into one small 'beaker'.

---

* * * *SUMMARY* * * *

Keats's main themes and ideas revolve around:

• negative capability and the ability to live with uncertainty

• liberality in morality which allow a poet to get closer to 'the untrodden regions of the mind'

• the meaning of love and his relationship with women

• dreams and the ideal in life and art

• poetry having beauty and intensity.

Critical approaches: 1817–2001

When Keats left instructions to have 'Here lies one whose name was writ in water' inscribed on his grave, he was reacting to the disappointment of public indifference: that his poetry had scarcely caused a ripple in the pool of contemporary literature. His once-calm confidence in the face of hostile criticism had

> **KEYWORD**
>
> Canon: the accepted 'classics', works and authors, traditionally studied at schools and universities.

been replaced by a bitter realization that his career would be cut off without having silenced and turned the doubters. But his resentment was a little exaggerated. Even if they did not sell particularly well, his works attracted much attention during his lifetime and in the immediate aftermath of his death. And if they sank into obscurity for a few years, his name eventually arose resplendent to be one of the most assured members of the English poetical **canon** by the end of the nineteenth century.

CONTEMPORARY CRITICISM: THE 'SHADOW OF PUBLIC THOUGHT'

The literary scene was dominated at the time by two famous journals whose pronouncements on taste significantly affected the reception given to writers. Like much else in the age, these journals were split along party lines, with the strongly conservative *Quarterly Review* having been set up in reaction to the predominantly liberal *Edinburgh Review*. The *Quarterly* supported the current Tory political establishment and was equally conservative in its literary views, for the most part condemning innovation; the *Edinburgh Review* was slightly more open to novelty (being generally in favour of Wordsworth for instance) – but it kept notably silent on Keats's poetry until he published his last volume, when a slightly condescending, but often favourable, review came in rather late in the day as far as Keats's career was concerned. By that time some serious damage had already been done by the hostile Tory press.

Keats hated the influence wielded by these heavyweight journals, noting that they had 'enervated and made indolent mens [*sic*] minds – few think for themselves' (*Letters*, 216). However, he professed himself indifferent to their vitriolic hostility, saying to his publisher, 'Praise or blame has but a momentary effect ... My own domestic criticism has given me pain without comparison beyond what Blackwood or the Quarterly could possibly inflict' (*Letters*, 155). Of course he regretted the detrimental effect on sales but he felt that 'the attempt to crush me in the Quarterly has only brought me more into notice'; his notoriety eventually meant that the legend of his life and poetry would live on. As he wrote to his brother: 'This is a mere matter of the moment – I think I shall be among the English Poets after my death' (*Letters*, 161).

POEMS (1817)

Of his first volume, Keats sardonically commented: 'it was read by some dozen of my friends who lik'd it; and some dozen who I was unacquainted with, who did not' (rejected Preface to *Endymion*). The work certainly did not sell and was largely ignored by the journals: only six reviews were written, some by Keats's own friends supporting it, others with an ominous taste of things to come. One magazine condemned him for his openly liberal 'political principles', while others warned him against the influence of Leigh Hunt on his style (see *Keats: The Critical Heritage*, ed. G. M. Matthews, Barnes and Noble, 1971, 69, 73). The volume itself was quite slight. Shelley had strongly advised Keats not to publish until he had a fuller body of verse to draw upon, and several reviews pointed out that Keats may come to regret this strident and somewhat immature collection. Keats's friend John Hamilton Reynolds, writing in the *Champion*, highlighted such exceptional examples of Keats's mature style as the sonnet 'On Chapman's Homer'. The volume also contained several politically inspired poems, as well as the open attack on Pope and the Augustan school of poetry in 'Sleep and Poetry'. These challenges to the political and literary establishments were noted even by journals who did not review the collection. They were, as yet, keeping their powder dry for future attacks.

ENDYMION (1818)

The single most harmful review of Keats's poetry – harmful because its circulation and influence was so large – appeared in the *Quarterly*. It was this famous critique of *Endymion* which many at the time blamed for Keats's untimely death, saying that it led to his consumption – or as Byron so memorably put it, ''Tis strange the mind, that very fiery particle,/ Should let itself be snuffed out by an Article' (*Don Juan*, XI, stanza 60).

The article itself was a scathing attack on Keats's *style* rather than the substance of *Endymion*. In fact it claimed that there is no substance to the poem: 'Mr Keats had advanced no dogmas which he was bound to support by examples; his nonsense therefore is quite gratuitous; he writes for its own sake.' The reviewer denounces this 'copyist of Mr Hunt' for his destruction of Pope's heroic couplet: 'There is hardly a complete couplet inclosing [sic] a complete idea in the whole book.' (*Keats: Narrative Poems, A Casebook*, ed. John Spencer Hill, Macmillan, 1983, 43, 44). However, it was obvious to readers at the time that the *Quarterly* was politically motivated in its damning and damaging censure.

The *Quarterly's* was not the most vicious attack. That distinction belongs to *Blackwood's Edinburgh Magazine*. Like the *Quarterly*, *Blackwood's* was a strongly Tory mouthpiece, but it was far more virulent and lively in its copy, often subjecting authors to satirical and witty attacks. Its chief target was Leigh Hunt whose own weekly magazine, the *Examiner*, consisted of a mixture of political commentary attacking the establishment, and original essays, reviews and poetry. It was here that Keats was first published – and, together with his public praise for the notorious Hunt, this context for his work meant that he was damned by association. A published poet, Hunt had been imprisoned in 1815 for attacking the Prince Regent in his magazine, and Keats's early verse not only followed the style of his idol but often specifically praised him as Libertas, champion of liberty.

Blackwood's gleefully picked up on the connection and decided, from its stance in Edinburgh, that Hunt was gathering a coterie of writers around him (amongst whom were included Keats's friend, Reynolds): it derisively labelled this group the 'Cockney School of Poetry', and went on to write a series of articles dedicated to mocking the loose style and even looser morals of the group.

When it came to Keats, *Blackwood's* had even better material as it uncovered his supposedly lower-class origins and the fact that he had been apprentice to an apothecary. In an age, observed the reviewer, when 'our very footmen compose tragedies' such impertinence in attempting something so far above himself as poetry must be condemned. The article concluded by sending this would-be poet 'back to the shop Mr John' and the patronizing label of little 'Johnny Keats' is one that would haunt the poet for the rest of his life and beyond (*Keats: Narrative Poems, A Casebook*, ed. John Spencer Hill, Macmillan, 1983, 41, 42).

POEMS (1820)

Keats's final collection was published two years after *Endymion* and exhibits all the hallmarks of a remarkable maturation. Described as 'one of the greatest single volumes of poetry of modern times' (*John Keats: Odes, A Casebook*, ed. G. S. Fraser, Macmillan, 1971, 15), it contains *Hyperion*, his romances and the great odes of 1819 – most of the poetry upon which his subsequent reputation has been built.

It was not universally recognized in his own day, many critics finding it 'laboriously obscure', much like his earlier work. What such reviewers often objected to (overtly at least) was such supposedly unintelligible phrases as 'a beaker full of the warm South' from an 'Ode to a Nightingale', expressions of **ellipsis** so characteristic of Keats as of his predecessor Shakespeare.

KEYWORD

Ellipsis: a type of poetic shorthand in which steps of logic are missed out in an effort to compress description.

As Keats's most recent biographer has pointed out, there was still an underlying political bias behind such judgements: 'He might have become a less obviously seditious and vulgar Cockney, but his idiom and versification were still dangerously unorthodox, his "paganism" was still undimmed, his vision of Classicism was still critical of present conditions, and his treatment of the theme of progress still defiantly liberal' (Andrew Motion, *Keats*, Faber and Faber, 1997, 524). Sales, possibly affected by his earlier critical mauling, were very poor, Keats's publishers still having copies of the original (small) print run on their hands eight years later – and this in an age when Byron's poetry sold by the thousands.

Not all reviewers and readers were negative. The *Edinburgh Review* finally broke its silence on Keats's work, its influential editor Francis Jeffrey weighing into the fray with a generally very positive review, including a measured defence of *Endymion*. John Scott, the liberal editor of the *London Magazine*, praised Keats and became so incensed in his defence of the poet against the cowardly (and anonymous) attacks in *Blackwood's* that he began a campaign against the journal. The campaign eventually led to a duel in which Scott was killed. Such high passions, typical of an age where literature and politics were followed far more fervently than they are today, certainly raised Keats's profile, even if they hardly boosted his sales. The damage had been done by the Tory heavyweights.

A 'POSTHUMOUS EXISTENCE'

As the news of Keats's death filtered back from Rome in March 1821, a whole new furore began. *Blackwood's* callously continued its series on the 'Cockney School' declaring that poets too weak to enter the fray should remain unpublished – a sentiment echoed by Lord Byron in the remarks quoted above. The myth that Keats had been killed by the article may have gained some currency from Keats's own friends who used this to attack the harsh remarks made by the Tory press.

However, it was Shelley who was the chief perpetrator. He wrote an elegy to Keats, '*Adonais*', in which he characterized the younger poet as a weak effeminate flower, not fitted to the hardships of life. This legend was to dominate critical thought for the next century or so, despite intermittent efforts by Keats's friends and later critics to 'rescue' the poet as a masculine and robust poet. With the critic Hazlitt, Byron and even Leigh Hunt adding remarks about Keats's 'effeminacy', either in style or lack of manly vigour, the legend grew.

'AMONG THE ENGLISH POETS': KEATS ENTERS THE CANON

It was not until 1848 that the rehabilitation of the poet had begun in earnest. For it was in that year that Richard Monckton Milnes, one of the 'Cambridge Apostles', published a biography of the poet. Along with fellow apostles, Arthur Hallam and Alfred Lord Tennyson, Milnes had long championed the work of Keats and Shelley over their far more celebrated contemporary Lord Byron. At first Tennyson's support merely brought the opprobrium of the Tory critics upon his own head. But as his fame and reputation grew, so Keats's did likewise.

Milnes's important and ground-breaking biography was in part meant as a corrective to the early reviews of the poet which had damned him by association with Leigh Hunt and the 'Cockney School'. By concealing many of Keats's liberal leanings a new myth began, one destined to outlast that of Shelley's wilting flower. This was the Keats who was apolitical, a Keats who fitted in with 'an emerging Victorian desire to escape from the harsh facts of social upheaval into leafy and respectable private luxury' (Motion, 575). It was in this guise that the pre-Raphaelites and then such exponents of Art-for-arts sake as Walter Pater and Swinburne could find such a champion. With his espousal of beauty above all else, and his creation of gorgeous medieval scenes, Keats was a natural forerunner for these causes.

IDEAS OR CLOSE READING?

At the beginning of the twentieth century, critics became interested in the philosophy and ideas behind Keats's poetry and tracked down many of the sources of the poet's allusions to and echoes of his predecessors, from the poetry of Wordsworth to the history books he had read at school; from his favourite Elizabethan poets to contemporary summaries of Greek myth. Whilst this helped confirm Keats as one of the most literary of writers (his reading forming a whole storehouse for his own poetical images), it also furnished grand ideologies upon which the poet is supposed to

KEYWORD

Neoplatonic: based on the ideas of Plato, this movement flourished in the Middle Ages and involved the theory that physical beauty was a sign of inward grace and spiritual beauty of the soul itself.

have structured his poems. The most favoured of these is the **Neoplatonic** search for an ideal, away from the actual world of 'fever and fret'. It can be found, if one looks, in poems as various as *Endymion* and the odes; and its chief critical advocates were Sidney Colvin, Clarence Thorpe and, later, Earl R. Wasserman.

With the growth of the New Criticism and the 'close reading' associated with F. R. Leavis and William Empson, came a new approach to Keats's work. Once again the poems proved fertile territory, with Keats's rich and often ambiguous style giving ample opportunities for the close and sophisticated scrutiny (ignoring such 'extraneous substance' as biography, reading and ideology) – typified by Empson's *Seven Types of Ambiguity* (Chatto and Windus, 1930) which brought some brilliant readings to bear on the poet's negatively capable work.

KEATS'S 'ANTI-ROMANCE'

In the early 1960s, a once-controversial reading of *The Eve of St Agnes* paved the way for a reassessment of Keats's supposedly escapist dreamworlds. In his essay, 'The Hoodwinking of Madeline', Jack Stillinger found an ironic distancing in the poem rather than the romantic idealism which earlier readers had been drawn to. Far from a sweet tale of love, *The Eve*, for Stillinger, is a story of scheming 'peeping Tomism', possibly rape on the part of the 'hero' Porphyro, and foolish belief in superstition and dreamworlds on the part of Madeline.

By including all the lavish details of romance and period setting, Keats was perhaps merely highlighting the anti-romantic nature of his story. The whole poem begins a move on the part of the poet away from idealism towards a more sceptical realism: from this point, claims Stillinger, 'dreaming is condemned'. (Jack Stillinger, 'The Hoodwinking of Madeline: Scepticism in "The Eve of St. Agnes"', *Studies in Philology*, 58 (1961); reproduced in John Spencer Hill (ed.), 164.)

BIOGRAPHICAL ANGLE: MACHO MAN OR MUMMY'S BOY?

Three great biographies were published in the 1960s, works which continue to exert a massive influence on Keats criticism. The first of these, Walter Jackson Bate's magisterial *John Keats* (Harvard University Press, 1963), provides an invaluable synthesis of the two approaches common in the early twentieth century. It brings to bear the skills of the close reader on the poems, while outlining the chief strands of the poet's thought as it developed over his lifetime.

Together with the meticulous Gittings (whose own biography was published by Heinemann in 1968), a far more manly 'Keats' is finally recovered. But, whereas the former finds masculinity as the chief merit of the later poetry, Gittings finds evidence of Keats's masculinity in other ways. Gittings's Keats, like many Regency youths (and indeed many in the decade Gittings was writing in!), was a sexual being, 'warmed with' more than one woman, and suffered first with syphilis and later with the unbearable knowledge that he should have 'had' Fanny Brawne whilst he was well enough to (*Letters*, 396).

Aileen Ward, meanwhile (John Keats: *The Making of a Poet*, Viking, 1963), was uncovering a Keats strongly influenced by events early in his life. Ward's is a **Freudian** interpretation of a poet who developed a strong Oedipal bond with his mother, only to

> ## KEYWORD
>
> **Freudian criticism:** a type of criticism which uses as its basis the psychoanalytical findings of Sigmund Freud. Freud wrote at the beginning of the twentieth century about the workings of the unconscious mind, the significance of early events in life, and the Oedipus complex – or the closeness of a boy's relations with his mother and the jealous desire to outdo the father.

be abandoned – and who bore the scars of that abandonment throughout his brief life. Ward, like many of the critics who have followed up her hints, did not fully develop the Freudian implications of this thesis. Ward refers to Freud only once in passing (p. 5) and Barbara Schapiro is one of the few critics to attempt a full exploration of what has recently been termed Keats's 'haunted psychic territory' (Wolfson, 2001, 114) – and that remains a rather unsubtle analysis, rather full of conjecture and 'uncovering' sexual imagery in the poetry (Barbara A. Schapiro, *The Romantic Mother: Narcissistic Patterns in Romantic Poetry*, Johns Hopkins University Press, 1983). A more convincing psychoanalytic account of the idealization of the feminine in Keats's thought is by Leon Waldoff, *Keats and the Silent Work of Imagination* (University of Illinois Press, 1985).

ADOLESCENT EMBARRASSMENT

During the 1970s one of the greatest general studies of the poet was produced, Stuart M. Sperry's masterly *Keats the Poet* (Princeton University Press, 1973). The decade also saw the publication of one of the more contentious pieces of Keats criticism, Christopher Ricks's

Keats and Embarrassment (Oxford University Press, 1974). Picking up on hints in an essay by John Bayley ('Keats and Reality'), Ricks argues that much of the best and most 'disconcerting' images created by the poet were those which had previously been condemned as immature and 'vulgar'.

Keats's verbal excesses capture an essential part of our human nature with more honesty than other more 'mature' poets, and Ricks charts the range from awkward embarrassment to the unselfconscious and often embarrass*ing*. Recently Marjorie Levinson has picked up on and extended the arguments of both critics (*Keats's Life of Allegory: The Origins of a Style*, Basil Blackwell, 1988) – although she challenges Ricks's view that Keats's 'badness' was part of a deliberate strategy. For Levinson, Keats's style, more concerned with embellishment and the allusions of the literary magpie than conveying serious themes, is associated not only with adolescent sexuality but with *arriviste* pretensions of the middle classes.

Levinson is one of the few critics to read the poet 'against the grain' – i.e. not taking Keats's strategy as a given, but **deconstructing** his intentions and noting his failures. Deconstruction and its predecessor, **Structuralism** did not make big waves in Keats criticism, although a David Lodge novel, *Small World* (Penguin, 1984), makes brilliant and witty play with *The Eve of St Agnes* as a paradigm for both these complex literary theories – as well as explaining them intelligibly for the lay reader, whilst telling a comic romance at the same time.

KEYWORDS

Deconstruction: a type of criticism, beginning with Jacques Derrida, in which critics 'locate the moment when a text transgresses the laws it appears to set up for itself' (see Raman Selden, *A Reader's Guide to Contemporary Literary Theory*, Harvester Press, 1985, 87).

Structuralism: an intellectual movement originating in France in the 1950s. Seeks to deny the authority of the author and to assert that all human endeavour (including literature) can be reduced to a series of signs or symbols.

New Historicism: a type of criticism which sees literature in its own context, whilst acknowledging that we can only ever view history as a projection of our own times.

NEW HISTORICISM

The subsequent fashion in literary criticism has had (and continues to exert) the most impact in recent years, causing an almost seismic shift in readings of the poet. For whilst it had been established fairly firmly in most readers' minds for well over a century that Keats was the most apolitical of poets, an inhabiter of dreamlands far removed from the cut and thrust of real life, suddenly the **New Historicist** movement uncovered a very different Keats, politically aware and regarded with suspicion by the Tory journals and general public alike – as a dangerous, potentially seditious and licentious poet, writing in a highly charged and highly politicised atmosphere.

For these New Historicist critics, contemporary criticism, notebooks, the journal of Leigh Hunt, events in the news whilst the poetry was being composed all suddenly became invaluable source materials for readings which found political implications in the least likely of places. The general conclusions have been that:

* Keats was recognized in his own day as a radical writer

* previously designated 'escapist' poems often contain responses to crises which were gripping the nation at the time (see Nicholas Roe's 'Keats's Commonwealth', *Keats and History*, ed. Nicholas Roe, Cambridge University Press, 1995, where he argues that 'To Autumn' is an indirect response to the bloody massacre at Peterloo)

* Keats was defined by his class – and often excluded from the world of letters inhabited by his more famous contemporaries.

Jerome J. McGann is often cited as the seminal influence on such readings with his important essay, 'Keats and the Historical Method in Literary Criticism' (*Modern Language Notes*, 94, 1979); together with Marilyn Butler's more general account of the period in *Romantics, Rebels and Reactionaries: English Literature and its Background 1760–1830* (Oxford University Press, 1982), McGann's study heralded a new approach to the poet. Keats's use of myth was found to be politically charged and even a seemingly traditional picture of country life such as 'To Autumn' had hidden resonances. The very 'gleaner' who steps so charmingly through the second stanza is a radical inclusion: for gleaning, the practice of picking up the left-over ears of wheat, had recently been outlawed, as the rich landowners protected their crops from any such old-fashioned acts of charity.

Other notable inclusions in this New Historicist account include:

* Daniel P. Watkins whose work (*Keats's Poetry and the Politics of the Imagination*, Farleigh Dickinson University Press, 1989) uncovers many of the class implications of the poetry

* John Barnard whose introduction to the poet's world as well as his poetry is both readable and informative and remains the best short study (*John Keats*, Cambridge University Press, 1987)

* Nicholas Roe's provocative and meticulously researched *John Keats and the Culture of Dissent* (Clarendon Press, 1997).

Collections of essays which explore similar themes include those edited by:

* Susan Wolfson (*Keats and Politics: A Forum, Studies in Romanticism*, 25, 1986, and more recently *The Cambridge Companion to Keats*, Cambridge University Press, 2001)

* Hermione de Almeida (*Critical Essays on John Keats*, Oxford University Press, 1991)

* Nicholas Roe (*Keats and History*, Cambridge University Press, 1995).

GENDER STUDIES

Ever since its first publication, Keats's poetry has often been associated with a feminine voice and thus makes an interesting case study in feminist criticism. How far can a male poet (especially one who made several sexist remarks in his own writings) be seen as a spokesman for female subjects?

In a series of articles, Susan Wolfson has done most to recover that early sense of the poet as an 'effeminate' writer in the eyes of such authoritative contemporary commentators as Shelley, Byron, William Hazlitt and Thomas De Quincey. Wolfson's articles and books include:

❋ 'Feminizing Keats', *Critical Essays on John Keats*, ed. Hermione de Almeida, Oxford University Press, 1991, 317–56

❋ 'Keats and the Manhood of the Poet', *European Romantic Review*, 6, 1995. Wolfson argues that this effeminate Keats (since so strongly denied in our own century) has a real basis in the poetry, in that Keats often plays with the idea of gender roles in his poems.

Other critics have focused on that core of Keatsian aesthetics, 'negative capability' finding this to be an 'anti-masculine conception of identity' (see Anne K. Mellor, *Romanticism and Gender*, New York, 1992, 174). In a chapter entitled 'Ideological Cross-Dressing' Mellor goes on to show that Keats 'locates poetic creation in the realm of the feminine, identifying it with pregnancy'.

Not all critics have been so generous in their depiction of Keats's relations with the feminine. Margaret Homans places Keats in the context of the largely female reading public of the time. She concludes that Keats remained hostile to the thought that he was writing for women and he 'makes of his poetry a masculine preserve, and in so doing he elects himself a member of the male club that poets in the classical tradition, and especially the high romantics, have always claimed literature to be, but which it is not' (Margaret Homans, 'Keats Reading Women, Women Reading Keats, *Studies in Romanticism*, 29, 1990, 341–70, 368). Other critics concur with her view that, in common with other male Romantic poets, Keats often appropriates or 'colonizes' a female voice, in what Anne Mellor terms 'a usurpation of female authority' (Mellor, 239) A sample of such critics may be found in *Romanticism and Feminism* (ed. Anne K. Mellor, Indiana University Press, 1988). In *Romanticism and Gender*, Anne Mellor herself tempers this idea by claiming that:

* Keats's appropriation of the feminine voice 'functions as an act of dependence and submission rather than of colonization and exploitation' (240)

* 'Occupying the position of a woman in the poetic discourse of the early nineteenth century was ... a source of anxiety for Keats' (179)

* 'His odes focus obsessively on female power' (182).

However, she concedes that Karen Swann is correct when she concludes that in such poems as 'La belle dame sans merci' Keats 'finally allied himself with the male against the female' because 'The male voice both appropriates and silences the female – we never hear what the *belle dame* thought or felt' (184).

---

* * *SUMMARY* * *

• Keats was at first either ignored or lampooned for his stylistic excess or his connection with Radical writers.

• His death was blamed (wrongly) on the viciousness of the critical attacks.

• His reputation was slow to rise, but did so spectacularly in the mid-nineteenth century.

• He has since been the darling of successive fashions of literary criticism, ranging from biographical to philosophical, close reading to New Historicism.

• New Historicist readings uncover the poet's relations with his politically turbulent times.

• Gender-based studies have found both feminism and misogyny in Keats's writings.

Where to next? 8

READ THE POEMS ...

READ THE POEMS ...

The first thing to do is to read the poems! This book deals with the more famous poems by Keats but such sonnets as 'Keen fitful gusts are wandering here and there' 'Bright Star' and 'On sitting down to read *King Lear* once again' also reward study – as does the revised version of *Hyperion* which Keats renamed 'The Fall of Hyperion'. Good selections exist in libraries and bookshops as well as fuller, more authoritative editions outlined below. Try to acquire one with detailed notes for some of the more obscure mythological references, biographical background and topical allusions. The poetry deserves such attention to detail though of course it can also be enjoyed without such critical paraphernalia.

... AND THE LETTERS

Some editions also include a selection of the letters which are perhaps as worthy of study as the poems. Separate and full editions of the letters are a good investment for the more serious student, especially for the notes they contain.

RESEARCH THE LIFE

Keats has been blessed with some excellent biographers, the most recent of whom is Andrew Motion. Like Stephen Coote's more concise 1995 biography, Motion sets the political scene, taking into account all the recent historical-critical work. Motion's study is very full with much critical opinion on the poetry itself.

For those interested in pursuing the biographical angle, it is often valuable to visit places Keats stayed when he composed certain poems. Armed with a biography and a copy of the poems, one might wish to follow the very walk around Winchester where Keats was inspired to compose 'To Autumn'; or sit in the garden of Keats's house in Hampstead on a May morning imagining him listening to nightingales. This house is open to the public and, like the house on the Spanish steps in Rome where he died, is well worth a visit, having been converted into a museum full of artefacts associated with the young poet.

READ THE CRITICS

Next it might be worth looking at some criticism. Several useful general introductions (of which John Barnard's *John Keats*, Cambridge University Press, 1987, is the most readable and interesting) as well as more complex critical studies are outlined in Chapter 7.

OTHER MEDIA

Of the numerous websites devoted to Romantic poetry the most useful are listed on *Romanticism on the Net* which can be found at www.users.ox.ac.uk/~scat0385/ Of these, the most informative is the Current Bibliography of the *Keats-Shelley Journal* (www.rc.umd.edu/reference/ksjbib/), which lists and comments on the most up-to-date scholarly articles and books on Keats and the poets and writers in his circle.

You will find taped readings of Keats's poems including the soon-to-be published Penguin *John Keats Selected Poems*, Audio Books. These may help the poetry to come alive.

EDITIONS OF KEATS'S POETRY

There are many useful collections of Keats's poems, including:

The Poems of John Keats, ed. Jack Stillinger, Harvard University Press, 1978; the authoritative version of the poems from which scholars generally quote. Excellent notes on the textual variations.

John Keats, ed. Elizabeth Cook, Oxford University Press, 1990; includes many of the important letters as well as useful notes and some of Keats's marginalia (the notes he made in his editions of Milton and Shakespeare). All of my quotations are from this edition.

Keats: Selected Poems and Letters, ed. Robert Gittings and Sandra Anstey, Heinemann, 1985; the best of the many available selections.

THE LETTERS

The Letters of John Keats, 1814–1821, ed. Hyder E. Rollins, 2 vols, Harvard University Press, 1958. The standard edition quoted by critics; also contains excellent notes. Unfortunately this is out of print and therefore only available in libraries.

The Letters of John Keats, ed. Robert Gittings, Oxford University Press, 1970, 1979; the best paperback edition, still in print.

Chronology of major works

1814 Publication of *Excursion*

1818 Publication of Keats's *Endymion*

1819 Writes 'La belle dame sans merci' and major odes including 'Ode to a Nightingale' and 'Ode on a Grecian Urn'; Keats writes ode 'To Autumn'

1820 Publication of Keats's *Lamia, Isabella, The Eve of St Agnes, and other Poems* (includes major odes)

GLOSSARY

Alliteration The repetition of consonants.

Assonance The echo of vowel sounds.

Augustan An era of English literature characterized by a reverence for all things classical, particularly the Latin literature of that period in Roman history when Augustus Caesar ruled (27 BC–AD 14). The English Augustans of the early–mid-eighteenth century favoured heroic couplets and well ordered verse.

Ballad A poem following the traditional form of a folk song, with regular rhyme-scheme and stanza length, often using repetition and telling a familiar tale.

Blank verse A style of poetry which has unrhymed lines of ten syllables each and employing the flowing rhythm natural to English. Used often by Shakespeare in his plays and, perhaps in its most sustained grandeur, by John Milton in his biblical epic, *Paradise Lost*.

Canon The accepted 'classics', works and authors, traditionally studied at schools and universities.

Deconstruction A type of criticism, beginning with Jacques Derrida, in which critics 'locate the moment when a text transgresses the laws it appears to set up for itself' (see Raman Selden, *A Reader's Guide to Contemporary Literary Theory*, Harvester Press, 1985, 87).

Ellipsis A type of poetic shorthand in which steps of logic are missed out in an effort to compress description.

End-stopped The opposite of enjambment; here the sense of the sentence requires a pause at the end of each line or couplet, giving a sense of containment, structure and order.

Enjambment A French word which describes the running on of one line of poetry into another, providing a sense of continuity, spontaneity and freedom.

Epic A long poem, detailing great heroic deeds. Some of the earliest recorded examples of this form are Homer's *The Iliad* and *The Odyssey*.

Freudian criticism A type of criticism which uses as its basis the psychoanalytical findings of Sigmund Freud. Freud wrote at the beginning of the twentieth century about the workings of the unconscious mind, the significance of early events in life, and the Oedipus complex – or the closeness of a boy's relations with his mother and the jealous desire to outdo the father.

Heroic couplets A style of poetry consisting of paired rhyming lines of ten syllables each.

Image A 'picture' created in the mind of the reader, often using sensory description. Consistent patterns of images, for instance on the subject of heat and cold, is known as imagery.

Lyric A brief poem often on a personal subject or one governed by a particular mood. Traditionally smooth and musical in rhythm like the lyrics to a song.

Metaphor The opposite of the literal. A comparison which instead of stating outright that something is *like* something else (as a simile does), *implies* the comparison by identifying the two things. When Keats says that he has 'travel'd in the realms of gold' he does not mean literal travel but metaphorical; he has read widely in the rich 'realms' of literature.

Neoplatonism Based on the ideas of Plato, this movement flourished in the Middle Ages and involved the theory that physical beauty was a sign of inward grace and spiritual beauty of the soul itself.

New Historicism A type of criticism which sees literature in its own context, whilst acknowledging that we can only ever view history as a projection of our own times.

Octet A unit of verse consisting of eight lines, generally with a self-contained rhyme-scheme.

Ode An elaborately constructed type of poem dating from classical times where it was traditionally a type of public address (almost like a hymn) which uses an exalted tone.

Onomatopoeia Words where the sound echoes the meaning, e.g. twitter, cuckoo, or (less obviously) murmur.

Oxymoron A type of paradox in which two opposite qualities are juxtaposed in a two-word phrase.

Paradox A statement which seems illogical, or self-contradictory but which contains an underlying truth.

Personification A device by which a quality, or a thing, or a non-human being is described or addressed as if a person.

Quatrain A unit of verse consisting of four lines, generally with a self-contained rhyme-scheme.

Rhyme-scheme A pattern of rhymed words linking the ends of lines together. Typical patterns include alternate rhyme-scheme (abab) where lines rhyme every other; and rhyming couplets (aabb) where pairs of consecutive lines rhyme.

Romanticism A movement in literature and the arts which began in the late eighteenth century, championing spontaneous and natural emotions above the rational, the formal, the civilized. British Romanticism is traditionally divided into a first generation of poets (of whom William Blake, William Wordsworth and Samuel Taylor Coleridge are the most studied) and a second generation (Lord Byron, Percy Shelley and John Keats).

Sonnet A poem of 14 ten-syllable lines, traditionally with a regular rhyme-scheme.

Spenserian stanzas Poetry consisting of a series of verses (or 'stanzas') of nine lines each with a repeated rhyme-scheme of ababbcbcc.

Structuralism An intellectual movement originating in France in the 1950s. Seeks to deny the authority of the author and to assert that all human endeavour (including literature) can be reduced to a series of signs or symbols.

FURTHER READING

Keats, John, *The Poems of Keats*, ed. Miriam Allott, Longman, 197●
    John Keats: The Complete Poems, ed. John Barnard, Penguin, 197.
    John Keats, ed. Elizabeth Cook, Oxford University Press, 199●
    The Letters of John Keats, ed. Robert Gittings, Oxford Universit
    Press, 1970, 1979

Barnard, John, *John Keats*, Cambridge University Press, 1987

Bate, Walter Jackson, *John Keats*, Harvard University Press, 1963

Bennett, Andrew, *Keats Narrative and Audience: The Posthumous Life o*
    Writing, Cambridge University Press, 1994

Butler, Marilyn, *Romantics, Rebels, and Reactionaries*, Oxford Universit
    Press, 1987

Coote, Stephen, *John Keats: A Life*, Hodder, 1995

De Almeida, Hermione, ed., *Critical Essays on John Keats*, G. K. Hall
    1990

Ford, George H., *Keats and the Victorians: A Study of His Influence an●*
    Rise to Fame 1821–1895, Yale University Press, 1944

Gittings, Robert, *John Keats*, Heinemann, 1968

Levinson, Marjorie, *Keats's Life of Allegory: The Origins of a Style*, Basi
    Blackwell, 1988

Matthews, G. M. ed., *Keats: The Critical Heritage*, Barnes and Noble
    1971

McGann, Jerome J., "Keats and the Historical Method in Literar
    Criticism" (1979)
    The Beauty of Inflections: Literary Investigations in Historica
    Method & Theory, Clarendon Press, 1988, 9–65

Mellor, Anne, *Romanticism & Gender*, Routledge, 1992
    ed. *Romanticism and Feminism*, Indiana University Press, 1988

Motion, Andrew, *Keats*, Faber and Faber, 1997

Ricks, Christopher, *Keats and Embarrassment*, Oxford University Press, 1976

Roe, Nicholas, *John Keats and the Culture of Dissent*, Clarendon Press, 1997
    ed. *Keats and History*, Cambridge University Press, 1994

Sperry, Stuart, *Keats the Poet*, Princeton University Press, 1973

Stillinger, Jack, *"The Hoodwinking of Madeline" and Other Essays on Keats's Poems*, University of Illinois Press, 1971

Vendler, Helen, *The Odes of Johns Keats*, Harvard University Press, 1983

Ward, Aileen, *John Keats: The Making of a Poet*, Viking, 1963

Wasserman, Earl R., *The Finer Tone: Keats' Major Poems*, John Hopkins University Press, 1953

Watkins, Daniel P., *Keats's Poetry and the Politics of the Imagination*, Farleigh Dickinson University Press, 1989

Wolfson, Susan, *The Questioning Presence: Wordsworth, Keats, and the Interrogative Mode in Romantic Poetry*, Cornell University Press, 1986
    ed. *Keats and Politics: A Forum. Studies in Romanticism* 25 (1986)

INDEX

Augustans, the 24, 37, 38, 64
Austen, Jane 16, 19

Barnard, John 74, 79
Bate, Walter Jackson 70
Bayley, John 57, 72
Blackwood's Magazine 64, 65, 66, 67
Blake, William 3, 16
Boccaccio, Giovanni 29
Bonaparte, Napoleon 14, 16, 23
Bowdler, Thomas 18
Brawne, Fanny 3, 11, 29, 30, 33–4, 47, 55
Burton, Richard 36
Butler, Marilyn 73
Byron, Lord 2, 3, 10, 18, 23, 25, 27, 36, 58, 64, 67, 68, 75

Castlereagh, Robert Stewart, Viscount 16
Champion, The 64
Chapman, George 21–3
Chartier, Alain 33
Clarke, Charles Cowden 10, 22, 60–1
Coleridge, Samuel Taylor 19, 23, 50
Colvin, Sidney 69
Conder, Josiah 54

Cook, Elizabeth 78
Coote, Stephen 77

Davy, Sir Humphrey 19
De Almeida, Hermione 74, 75
deconstruction 72
De Quincey, Thomas 75
Donne, John 7

Eclectic Review, The 54
Edinburgh Review, The 63, 67
Elgin, Lord 28
Eliot, T.S. 7, 50
Empson, William 69
Evert, W.H. 37
Examiner, The 10, 18–19, 65

Fraser, G.S. 66
French Revolution, the 14–15, 16–17, 18, 19, 28, 51, 54
Freud, Sigmund 71

gender 54–6, 74–6
George IV, Prince Regent 16, 65
Gittings, Robert 70–1, 79
Guy's Hospital 10

Hallam, Arthur 68
Hazlitt, William 11, 68, 75

Herder, Johann 28
Hill, John Spencer 65, 66, 70
Homans, Margaret 75
Homer 21–3
Hunt, Henry 18
Hunt, Leigh 10, 11, 12, 16, 17, 18, 21, 64, 65, 66, 68, 73

Jeffrey, Francis 67

Keats, Frances (Keats's mother) 10, 55, 71
Keats, Frances (Keats's sister) 10
Keats, George (Keats's brother) 10
Keats, John *passim*
Keats, Thomas (Keats's father) 10
Keats, Tom (Keats's brother) 10, 12, 27
King George III 16

Leavis, F.R. 69
Levinson, Marjorie 57, 72
Lodge, David 72
London Magazine, The 67

McEwan, Ian 1
McGann, Jerome 73–4
Mellor, Anne 75–6

Milnes, Richard Monckton 68

Milton, John 2, 21, 23,
    38, 58
Motion, Andrew 1, 67,
    68, 77
mythology 23–9,
    39–40, 41, 43

negative capability
    50–2
New Historicism 72–4

Paine, Thomas 16
Pater, Walter 68
Peterloo Massacre 18
Pitt, William the
    Younger 15
Pope, Alexander 22,
    64, 65
Priestley, Joseph 19

Quarterly Review, The
    63, 64, 65

Reynolds, John
    Hamilton 64, 66
Ricks, Christopher 57,
    71–2
Roe, Nicholas 73, 74
Romantic movement
    2–3, 11, 20, 23, 50, 53
Rousseau, Jean-Jacques
    14

Schapiro, Barbara 71
Schlegel, August 28
Scott, John 67
Scott, Sir Walter 10, 19
Severn, Joseph 12

Shakespeare, William
    3, 10, 18, 50, 53, 54,
    66
Shelley, Percy 2, 3, 18,
    28, 41, 50, 51, 61, 64,
    68, 75
Southey, Robert 10
Spenser, Edmund 2,
    10, 21, 38
Sperry, Stuart 71
Stillinger, Jack 32, 69,
    70, 78
Stoppard, Tom 1
structualism 72
Swann, Karen 76
Swinburne, Algernon
    68

Tennyson, Alfred, Lord
    68
Thorpe, Clarence 69

Voltaire 14

Waldoff, Leon 71
Ward, Aileen 55, 70, 71
Wasserman, Earl R. 69
Watkins, Daniel P. 74
Wedgwood, Josiah 19
Wellington, Duke of
    17
Winckelmann, Johann
    28
Wolfson, Susan 71,
    74–5
Wordsworth, William
    2, 3, 11, 15, 23, 41, 50,
    53, 54, 63, 69

Works of Keats
    Endymion 23–4
        27, 28–9, 48, 54,
        56, 58, 65, 67, 69
    Eve of St. Agnes, The
        2, 4, 30–3, 34, 36,
        38, 40, 42, 44, 46, 53,
        55, 58, 69, 72
    'Fancy' 58
    Hyperion 2, 4–5, 11,
        23, 24–9, 36, 38, 46,
        47, 56, 66
    Isabella; or the Pot of
        Basil 29–30, 36, 60
    'La belle dame sans
        merci' 4, 8, 33–5,
        44, 56, 60
    Lamia 2, 4, 8, 35–8,
        52, 54, 55, 58–9, 60
    'Ode on a Grecian
        Urn' 8, 43–5,
        54–5, 59
    'Ode on Melancholy'
        45–7, 48, 55, 61, 62
    'Ode to a
        Nightingale'
        40–1, 44, 46, 47,
        58, 61, 66
    'Ode to Psyche'
        38–40, 41, 55
    'On First Looking
        into Chapman's
        Homer' 21–3, 28,
        64
    'Sleep and Poetry'
        54, 57–8, 64
    'To Autumn' 8,
        47–9, 78